HULLABALOO!

YoungWriters

SOUTH YORKSHIRE

Edited by Chris Hallam

First published in Great Britain in 2003 by
YOUNG WRITERS
Remus House,
Coltsfoot Drive,
Peterborough, PE2 9JX
Telephone (01733) 890066

SB ISBN 1 84460 229 X

FOREWORD

Young Writers was established in 1991 as a foundation for promoting the reading and writing of poetry amongst children and young adults. Today it continues this quest and proceeds to nurture and guide the writing talents of today's youth.

From this year's competition Young Writers is proud to present a showcase of the best poetic talent from across the UK. Each hand-picked poem has been carefully chosen from over 66,000 'Hullabaloo!' entries to be published in this, our eleventh primary school series.

This year in particular we have been wholeheartedly impressed with the quality of entries received. The thought, effort, imagination and hard work put into each poem impressed us all and once again the task of editing was a difficult but enjoyable experience.

We hope you are as pleased as we are with the final selection and that you and your family will continue to be entertained with *Hullabaloo! South Yorkshire* for many years to come.

CONTENTS

Dearne Carrfield Primary School

Laura Green (10)	62
Lauren Marsh (10)	63
Emily Morris (9)	63
Joshua Oskinski (8)	64
Leigh Jones (9)	64
Brogan Hough (8)	65
Barry Pugh (8)	65
Kirsty Booth (9)	66
Sarah Gauntley (9)	66
Chloe Nolan (8)	67
Kyle Frost (8)	68
James Chambers (9)	69
Charlotte Arundell (8)	69
Sophie Thompson (7)	70
Nathan Thompson (8)	70
Aiden Cooper (9)	71
Rebecca Stocks (8)	71
Eden Shortt (8)	72
Janina Sills (8)	72
Jordan Ratcliffe (9)	73
Vanessa Minshull (8)	73
Ellie McCrystal (8)	74
Joshua Marsh (8)	74
Charlie Ludlam (8)	75
Jasmine Hopper (9)	75
Katrina Pugh (9)	76
Jasmine Hall (10)	76
Brandon Crook & Patrick Desbrough (10)	77
Jordan Clark (10)	78
Cody Mellor (9)	79
Katie Jackson (9)	79
Rebecca Orton (10)	80
Sarah Cavell (10)	80

Ferham Primary School

Rachel Boam (11)	81

Greystones Primary School

Frances Hughes (10)	81

Holy Rood RC Primary School

Angela Walker (9)	82
Hannah Gregson (9)	82
Rebecca Wilkin (9)	83
Thomas Keating (9)	83

Hoyland Common Primary School

Chantelle Beet (9)	84
Tamsin O'Brien (9)	85
Bethany O'Brien (9)	86
Lorna Welch (8)	86
Brett Jubb (9)	88
Alex Owen (9)	88
Joe Greenhough (8)	89
Joseph Platts (8)	89
Jake Adams (8)	90
Laura Wood (9)	92
Kimberley Sayles (10)	93
Elisabeth Platts (9)	93
Sophie Adderley (10)	94
Tyler Vaines (9)	94
Liam Birks (10)	95
Sam Westerman (10)	95
Melissa Erwin (9)	96
Siobhan Ritchie (10)	96
John Werboweckjy (11)	97
Ashley Burkinshaw (10)	97
Matthew Smith (10)	98
David Longford (10)	98
Corey Sadler-Knott (10)	99
Sarah Hirst (11)	99
Tanya Robinson (10)	100
Lindsey Whitmore (10)	100
Jonathan Owen (11)	101
Sheridan Griffiths (10)	101
Rhiannon Sharp (9)	102
Kelsey Green (10)	102
Jamie Gardner (9)	103
Amy Bramley (9)	103

Bridie Mayock (8)	104
Eden Turner (8)	104
Rebekkah Loczki (9)	105
Katie Cross (10)	105
Ryan Burdin (9)	106
Katie Derbyshire (11)	106
Charlotte Aimee Robinson (10)	107
Nicola Davies (10)	107
Luke Micklethwaite (10)	108
Elliott Parker (10)	109
Lauren Cross (7)	110
Jessica Mellars (7)	111
Amy Louise Rooney (8)	111
Jacob Bellamy (7)	112
Samantha Sidebottom (8)	112
Sam Birtles (8)	112
Georgia Evans (8)	113
Brooke Green (8)	113
Carly Hogan (8)	114
Billy Evans (7)	114
Shannon Harris (8)	115
Bradley Thornton (7)	115
Rheanna Hall (7)	116
Sophie Hodson (7)	118
Robert Crowther (8)	118
Adam Hinkles (9)	118
Aiden Birks (8)	119
Ashley Sanderson (9)	119
Hollie Sylvester (8)	120
Robbin Evans (9)	121
Amelia Goodair (8)	122
Natalie Briscoe (8)	123
Sarah Newbold (9)	125
Chloe Levers (8)	126
Kyle Reese Thomas (11)	127
Ian Uttley (10)	127
Ben McNamara (10)	128
Stacey Jayne Rooney (10)	128

Monique Norcliffe (11)	182
Jenny Griffin (10)	182
Jordan Feetham (10)	183
Jade Poole (11)	184
Bradley Bradshaw (11)	185
Amanda Caesar (11)	186
Emma White (11)	187
Luke Platts (11)	187
Chloe Lomas (10)	188
Emily Biney (10)	189
Whitney Hill (10)	189
Pasha Adele Ankers (10)	190
Charlotte Linfitt (11)	190
Terri Adkins (11)	191
Jade Lawson (11)	192

Southfield Primary School

Loren Turner (10)	192

Trinity Croft CE (A) School

Rachel Taylor (11)	193
Nicole Cox (11)	193
Robin Stanley (10)	194
Bethan Middlemiss (10)	194
Travis Cant (11)	195
Luke Wagstaff (10)	195

Victoria Primary School

Jessica Connelly (10)	196
Brian Gillmore (11)	196
Ashleigh Campbell (8)	197

Woodthorpe School

Connah Hunter (8)	197
Emira Essalah (9)	198

The Poems

ON MY WAY HOME

Under the tree,
under the leaves, life starts to wake.
Roots turn to snakes trying to break
from their prison of mud.
Sky painted with leaves.
Cut grass have races in the wind.
But me, I'm just on my way home,
through the wind, swimming in oceans
of shadows.
I've been blown into a jungle
of flowers.
It's silent here, all the sounds have
drowned, apart from the rustling of me
on my way home.
The wind is speaking to me, words I
don't understand.
Everyone is alive apart from me.
I'm just going home.

Elizabeth Perryman (9)

THE ROLLER COASTER

The roller coaster goes up slowly
when it's at the top it flies down fast.
People scream! Hold on tight.
Some put their hands up in the air.
They've been on before.
Round the corner. Tips sideways.
Straps to keep in your place.
Upside down in a circle.
Dizzy. Throw up. *Euugh!*
Twists around the bend.
Think we'll bang into the fence.
Zoom round the corner.
Slows down.
Stops.
You get off. Others get on.

Carl Marsden (10), Daniel Kelly (11)
Geneane Connell & Matthew Varnham (11)
Abbey School

RIDES

Roller coaster going up and down
round and round and upside down.
Get strapped in and hold on tight.
Dodgem cars bumping, jolting.
Heads wobbling, makes me dizzy.
Big wheel takes you up to the sky.
Feels like you're never going to stop going up high.
Pirate ship whooshing up and down
makes my tummy feel funny, makes me scream.
Ghost train going through the doors.
Dark and scary, zombies, bats.
Something touched me, oh what was that?
I like rides because they make me feel,
happy, excited and sometimes even scared.

Daniel Gilbert (10) Gemma York, Lily Todd (11)
& Rachael Lindley (12)
Abbey School

Mr Lubba Lubba

A funny person with funny legs
walks home -
wibble wobble, wibble wobble.
Slipping along on ice
Arggggh! Dush!
Head aches,
bottom's numb,
legs cut and bruised.
His name is Mr Lubba Lubba.
He lives in cuckoo land.
Cuckoo, cuckoo, cuckoo.
His door is number four.
Bang, crash, slam, ouch!
He caught his finger in the door.
Neighbour's complaining, 'Too much noise!'
What a hullabaloo.

Maxine Young (10) Robert Wardale (11)
Carla Higgins (11) & Briony Burgin
Abbey School

THE WAR BANANA

I am a banana yellow and ripe
Born in America's south
An English soldier
Stole me away
In ration time - Yorkshire south.

For his little niece
Who'd never seen
A fruit so yellow
From a place not seen.

She took me to school
They passed me around
Around, around
Around, around.

No longer yellow
Soggy and brown
Beri's grandma's gift
In a war-time town.

Beri May Allen-Miller (9)
Anston Brook Primary School

DADDY LOVE

Daddy smacks when I am naughty,
Daddy shouts when I am bad,
Daddy screams when I am annoying,
Daddy punishes when I am harassing,
But when I'm good Daddy gives me
Daddy love.

Rebecca Amber Rose Dabill (9)
Anston Brook Primary School

EXPLORATIONS

As I swim to the bottom of the dark deep sea
A bulging treasure chest I do see.

I tried to open it but ran out of breath
I swam to the surface to avoid my death.

I held my breath, dived and thought of gold
The treasure chest I then did hold.

The exterior of the sea came into sight;
I had an idea of fortune and fame
But as you don't know me, this was just a game.

Sam Holland (9)
Anston Brook Primary School

TEACHERS

This is what teachers say:
'No shouting,'
'No screaming,'
'Put your pencils down,'
'Stop fighting.'
That's what they say.

This is what teachers do:
They pull their hair out,
Scream at us,
Shout at other teachers.
That's what they do.

Laura Tomlinson (10)
Anston Brook Primary School

I Saw

I saw a dog in the park,
He wagged his tail and started to bark.
I saw a cat chase a mouse, she grabbed its tail
And brought it in the house.
I saw the mouse get away
And live to play another day.

Lucy Reaney (8)
Anston Brook Primary School

If I Was An Animal In A Zoo!

If I was an animal in a zoo,
I'd have no privacy to go to the loo!
If I was an animal in a zoo,
Children would stare at me and other animals too.
If I was an animal in a zoo,
I wouldn't get eaten by lions or tigers.
If I was an animal in a zoo,
I'd wish to be free and play in the sun.
I'd wish I was swinging from trees in the jungle.
If I was an animal in a zoo,
I'd be bored all day and wish I was home.

Jamie Self (10)
Anston Brook Primary School

DOLPHINS

Dolphins jumping in and out of the water.
Splashing and sploshing in groups called schools.
Some have a long beak and have up to 260 teeth.
Dolphins love water, they are so graceful.
They are so good at diving.

I think I like dolphins.

Dolphins diving deep below the surface seeing sharks and salmon!
Eating and gobbling up all the fish.
One big dive out and back into the water, it is so much fun.
I think I would like to be a dolphin, would you?

I think I like dolphins, *yeah!*

Madeline Smith (8)
Anston Brook Primary School

LOVE

Love brings happiness into your life,
Love makes a flower bloom,
Love is for me and you,
What is love? A way to make new friends,
Love is what God has shown us,
What is love . . . ?

April Elliott (9)
Anston Brook Primary School

LOVE IS . . .

Love is all around us,
Love is everywhere,
Love is inside us,
I'm sure about that.

Love is a newborn baby,
Love is a favourite teddy,
Love is having friends,
Love is spending time with your family.

Gemma Fox (9)
Anston Brook Primary School

THE THREE WISHES

I wish my room was always tidy,
I wish everything could tidy itself away,
I wish that it could snow on Christmas,
Why don't any of these ever work out?

Welcome to the real world!

Suzanne Machin (10) & Rebekah Jory (9)
Anston Brook Primary School

MUM

Mum is fab,
Mum can bake,
Mum makes you better,
When you've got a headache.

Mum is jolly,
Mum is funny,
Although she spends,
A lot of money.

Mum is lovely,
Mum is sweet,
Mum makes you wash,
Your sweaty feet.

Mum buys clothes,
Mum buys toys,
Mum can't get enough,
Of her two little boys.

Ashley Bullement
Ballifield Primary School

IF

If I were my pussy cat
I would drink milk
Stretch my long ginger body
And sharpen my long claws . . .
Every day.

If I were my house
I would stand up proud
After watching the children laugh and shout
That tickles . . .
Every day.

If I were my mum
I would get up promising not to shout
Drop my kids off at school
With a lively hug . . .
Every day.

If I were my car
I would zoom along the land
Doing 50 miles per hour
Parking up, being lonely . . .
Every day.

If I were my brother
I would go to nursery
Do a painting of my mum
Eat my snack, go out to play . . .
Every day.

But I am glad - that I am me.
Are you glad that you are you?
I know a secret
Have a guess . . .
Everybody's *special.*

Freya Stennett (10)
Ballifield Primary School

MY TEDDY

I take my teddy everywhere,
Together at night we climb the stairs,
She joins me when I say a prayer
And she hugs me to show she cares.

I take my teddy everywhere,
We wake up early,
With her hair tight and curly,
Her small brown eyes are round and pearly.

I take my teddy everywhere,
Deep in her chest is a red, red heart,
To me she is a precious bear,
We dance all night in my dream.

Eleanor Swallow (10)
Ballifield Primary School

YOU LOST THE GAME

You lost the game!
You lost the *game!*
Do you feel any shame?

Do *not* disclaim
You lost the game
I'm not to blame,
Oh, curse your name.

You lost the game!
You lost the *game!*
Do you feel any shame?

Your aim was lame,
Your play was tame,
You deserve the shame,
You lost the *game.*

You lost the game!
You lost the *game!*
Do you feel any shame?

Your play's the same,
The chances came,
How can you claim footballing fame?
You lost the game!

Isabel Dickens (11)
Carterknowle Junior School

THE REF

Ref, ref,
You're the best,
You're way better than the rest.

Ref, ref,
He's the best,
But he's always a lousy pest,
He never welcomes his football guest,
But ref, he never gets the rest.

Ref, ref,
You're the best,
You're way better
Than the rest.

Chamin Khan (11)
Carterknowle Junior School

SO BEEFY BIG AND TALL

As big as an elephant and twice as tall,
He's gone and kicked it over the wall.

When he first walked out, we all felt small,
He's so tall, he has to crawl,
When he goes through the hall.

As big as an elephant and twice as tall,
He's gone and kicked it over the wall.

Don't fall, Paul,
Just kick the ball,
Noooooo! *Not over the stadium wall!*

As big as an elephant and twice as tall,
He's gone and kicked it over the wall.

Roseanna Bryan (11)
Carterknowle Junior School

THE PLAYERS AND THE CROWD

Pass the ball, pass the ball, pass the ball,
You idiot.
Pass the ball, pass the ball, pass the ball,
You fool.
Don't worry the game is not over yet,
We can still score, yes I bet,
If we don't win, we will regret.

Pass the ball, pass the ball, pass the ball,
You idiot.
Pass the ball, pass the ball, pass the ball,
You fool.

Pass the ball, pass the ball, pass the ball,
You idiot.
Pass the ball, pass the ball, pass the ball,
You fool.

Julie Hallatt (10)
Carterknowle Junior School

MANAGERS

Shoot, there's a player behind you,
Behind you, behind you.
Shoot, there's a player behind you,
Behind you, behind you, *shoot!*
You might be better trying to draw,
Why don't you go and score?
Shoot, there's a player behind you,
Behind you, behind you,
Shoot, there's a player behind you,
Behind you, behind you,
Why don't you sit on the floor
And eat an apple right to the core?
Shoot there's a player behind you,
Behind you, behind you,
Shoot, there's a player behind you,
Behind you, behind you,
Shoot!

Andy Moss (11)
Carterknowle Junior School

THE DRAGON

In a cave upon a hill,
There was a dragon who liked to kill.
All the people were scared to death,
But not a girl who's name was Beth.
One day, Beth climbed the dragon's hill,
When the dragon saw her he said, 'What a perfect kill!'
The dragon found his colossal pot
And left it till it was boiling hot.
A few minutes later when Beth was at the top,
The villagers heard a ginormous chop.
Poor little Beth was never seen again
And the villagers wrote her will in a dragon pen.

Xanthe Dodds (9)
Carterknowle Junior School

DRINK AND DRIVE

Have you ever had some beer
And said, 'Can I have more here?'
Then did you go out of the bar
And go home in your brand new car?
But then did you have a very big crash
And you had to pay lots of cash?
Instead of getting stung by bees from a beehive,
I would rather not drink and drive.

Have you ever had some wine
And said, 'Yes please, more would be fine?'
Then did you topple out of your friend's home
And trip over a garden gnome?
But that journey back on your motorbike,
Hurt someone more than you would like.
Instead of getting stung by bees from a beehive,
I would rather not drink and drive.

Martha Snow (9)
Carterknowle Junior School

CATS!

An owner lover
A road runner
A fish eater
A mouse killer
A leg attacker
A bed climber
A chair warmer
A wallpaper scratcher
A face licker
A toilet sipper
A dog hater
A cat fighter
A toe biter
A sock hider
A litter filler.

Debra Cranwell (10)
Carterknowle Junior School

MY PET ALIEN

My pet alien
Is big and hairy,
On a dark night
He's really scary.

My pet alien
Is yellow and green,
I want him to be nice
Instead he's mean.

My pet alien
Is not very nice,
His diet consists of
Mushed up mice!

My pet alien
Is really quite kind,
That's why he's the best pet
You'll ever find!

Natalia Mole (9)
Carterknowle Junior School

HORRIBLE SCHOOL DINNERS

Bumpy custard,
Lumpy custard,
Wet broccoli too.

Hot custard,
Cold custard,
Meatball stew.

Wet custard,
Dry custard,
It's horrible goo.

I've finished my poem,
So now it's your turn
To make me the *winner!*

Danielle Smart (9)
Carterknowle Junior School

SCOOBY-DOO

Scooby-Doo and his friend Shaggy are
Total scaredy-clown's when Shaggy
Screams when he sees ghosts, he feels
Like saying nouns.

The rest of the gang make plans and
Always do their best, when Fred and
Daphne make plans and always take
Some rest.

At last the mystery is solved, thanks to
Mystery Inc and they're always forever grateful
That they're never going to shrink.

Rachael Atkinson (8)
Carterknowle Junior School

CD PLAYER

A noise maker
An entertainer
A headache maker
A cog-holder
A music player
A disc-spinner
A time-waster
A button presser
A light giver
A neighbour annoyer
A vibrator
A pet scarer.

What is it . . . ?

Leah Boyle (10)
Carterknowle Junior School

WASHING MACHINE

A loud rumbler
A soap eater
A clothes washer
A fast spinner
A sock loser
A dirty-kids horror
A water waster
An odour-eater
A clothes shrinker
A gorgeous smeller
A blob of mud's worst enemy.

Anna Leicester (10)
Carterknowle Junior School

TV

A loud buzzer
A children's lover
A horror for Mother
A time waster
An educator
An entertainer
A zombie maker
A money waster
A fashion taster
An electric talker
A bright picture
A late night caller.

Heather Hutchings (10)
Carterknowle Junior School

FOOD

Who is it likes mushy peas?
How about Molly?
Molly likes lolly.
How about Sam?
Sam likes jam.
How about Jade?
Jade likes marmalade.
How about Jake?
Jake likes cake.
How about Kelly?
Kelly likes jelly.
How about Akash?
Akash like mash.
How about Pips?
Pips likes chips.
How about Pete?
Pete likes meat.
How about Audrey?
Audrey like strawberry.

Emma Brown (10)
Carterknowle Junior School

MUM'S PLANTS

Rosie, Bright, Shiny and Baby
Are all Mum's plants.
Rosie is tall,
Bright is middle,
Shiny is tall too
And Baby is small.

Ev'ry day they all like to say,
'Good morning, good morning'
And sometimes at night
They like to say, 'Goodnight.'
It's always fun to say hello
When you pop in.

Iona McEwan (7)
Carterknowle Junior School

THE MONSTER

The monster always is hungry
And he's usually very tickly.
He's as tall as a tree,
Much taller than me
And he gives me a fright
In the night.
He's very brave and
He lives in a cave
With his monstrous children
And wife.
He eats his tea much faster
Than me
And he only eats with a knife.

Torran McEwan (7)
Carterknowle Junior School

HEDGEHOGS

Hedgehogs are spiky,
They eat dog food and mice
When they're scared, they roll up into little balls.
Hedgehogs have furry bellies which are soft and nice.
They aren't very big and only
Come out at night,
That's when they eat.
Hedgehogs don't like the light.

Holly Gillan (9)
Carterknowle Junior School

MOONLIGHT ANIMALS

I sat in my bed,
It was a quiet night,
The moon was shining,
A silvery light.

The silvery lightness,
Danced around,
It took me with it,
Right to the ground!

Then a shadow
Came into the light!
What could it be?
It was a great kite!

It started to dance!
It gave a small frown,
With its elegant neck up
And its pretty tail down.

Then all kinds of animals,
Reptiles and mammals pranced,
They elegantly, beautifully,
Lightly danced.

Munya Redman-Bayasi (8)
Carterknowle Junior School

IT JUST DIDN'T WORK

I tried the singing
I tried the art
I tried the woodcraft
I tried being smart
But it just didn't work.

I tried the dressing
I tried the sewing
I tried the dancing
I tried the glowing
But it just didn't work.

I tried the hairdressing
I tried the cooking
I tried the make-up
I tried the looking
But it just didn't work.

Grace Procter (8)
Carterknowle Junior School

LOVE

Love is cherry red
It smells like a perfumed flower,
Love tastes sweet and crisp,
It sounds like a hummingbird singing,
It feels as silky as a feather.
Love lives in the heart of gold.

Samuel Humphries (10)
Conisbrough Balby Street J&I School

THE SOLAR SYSTEM

G iant planets swirling like a hurricane.
A stronauts come with flags and land on different planets.
L ayers and layers of stars all around us.
A liens sleeping in their wondrous beds.
X ray glasses to see all the flashes.
Y ou can see a black hole leading to a different solar system.

Aiden Forster (10)
Conisbrough Balby Street J&I School

A YOUNG BOY FROM LEICESTER

There was a young boy from Leicester,
Who played the role of a jester,
He danced and pranced in shops
Until the woman called the cops,
That little disaster from Leicester.

Oliver Rigby (11)
Conisbrough Balby Street J&I School

MY GRANDADS

G randads are very special,
R emote controls are their favourite,
A nnoying me, they like the best,
N utty and mad at times,
D o your head in lots,
A lthough I love him, he's the best,
D oes his very best to make me happy,
S illy grandads are better than the rest.

Kirstie Anne Hawley (11)
Conisbrough Balby Street J&I School

MY HOBBY FOOTBALL

The whistle blows, the game is off.
Thrashing bodies scamper about the field like armies of ants.
Pushing, scrambling to score the goals.
Weather changing, tempers rising.
Colours, numbers catch the attention of many beady eyes.
Tackling, hat tricks, skills saving the ball.
Noise erupting like a volcano spilling over.
Time passes, the clock ticks like a bomb.
The whistle blows and the game is over.

Kirsty Smith (10)
Conisbrough Balby Street J&I School

MY RABBITS

My rabbits are black and white,
But be careful, they might bite.

Through the day they gnaw the hutch,
But at night, they don't do much.

Big eyes, small nose,
Sometimes they do a little pose.

My brother says they're very nice,
Especially served as curry and rice.

Touch them if he dare,
For they're mine to love and care.

Kirsty Rew (11)
Conisbrough Balby Street J&I School

ICE

Look, look at the ice,
It shines like the moon.
You are as smooth as a polished table.
Sparkling, glittering in the moonlit sky.
You can make black ice.

Ice, ice, ice,
Ice, ice,
Ice.

Rachael Colton (8)
Dalton Listerdale J&I School

MY SENSES

I like the look of milk,
waving like the sea.

I like the feel of hot chocolate,
burning the air.

I like the taste of pictures,
just been painted.

I like the smell of bees,
swaying their wings.

I like the sound of sand,
playing with their friends.

Kori Skene (8)
Dalton Listerdale J&I School

SENSES

I like the look of sweets,
unwrapping themselves.

I like the feel of sunshine,
in the breeze.

I like the taste of flowers,
twisting their heads.

I like the smell of birds,
in the wavy tree.

I like the sound of fur,
whistling through he wind.

Clare Baldi (8)
Dalton Listerdale J&I School

I LIKE IT

I like the look of beans,
bubbling on my hand.

I like the feel of petrol,
running down my skin.

I like the taste of oranges
and nibbling in the air.

I like the smell of grass,
wafting its song.

I like the sound of globes,
jumping and smashing.

Joshua Booth (8)
Dalton Listerdale J&I School

SENSES

I like the look of music
filling up the air.

I like the feel of sausages
melting in my mouth.

I like the taste of fur
tingling up my arm.

I like the smell of the blotched sun
filling the sky with light.

I like the sound of petrol
pounding down the engine pipes.

Curtis Benton (8)
Dalton Listerdale J&I School

I LIKE

I like the look of fire
        melting me like a candle.

I like the feel of the sunshine
        beaming down on my skin.

I like the taste of thunder
        shouting inside me.

I like the smell of sheep
        dancing in the field.

I like the sound of birds
        chirping away in the treetop.

Alex Hickman (8)
Dalton Listerdale J&I School

I LIKE

I like the look of apples,
                jumping over the clouds.

I like the feel of carpets,
                swishing on a star.

I like the taste of gravy,
                bubbling on the sun.

I like the smell of lambs,
                flying on the moon.

I like the sound of helicopters,
                whistling in the sea.

Thomas Coy (9)
Dalton Listerdale J&I School

SENSES

I like the look of crisps,
        melting in a hot desert.

I like the feel of daffodils,
        touching my deserted hand.

I like the taste of water features,
        gliding into a big waterfall.

I like the smell of radios,
        songs floating up in the air.

I like the sound of fluff,
        rustling around in the light planet.

Elliot Ralph (8)
Dalton Listerdale J&I School

ME

I like the look of fizzy pop,
            running down my spine.

I like the feel of music,
            flying around my head.

I like the taste of dogs,
            howling at night.

I like the smell of trees,
            singing their song.

I like the sound of sweets,
            marching around my body.

Jack Sharpe (8)
Dalton Listerdale J&I School

FIREWORK

Blazing light springs up in the air,
Exploding as loud as Concorde,
Glimmering up as high as stars,
Now it's really hot and ready to blow,
Then a blazing glow as bright as the sun,
Now it blows with a loud
Boom!

Mark Proctor (8)
Dalton Listerdale J&I School

MY SENSES

I like the look of sofas,
          waiting in the room.

I like the feel of chips,
          to finger in my hand.

I like the taste of recorders,
          as my mouth bites the tip.

I like the smell of pictures,
          fragrant on the wall.

I like the sound of chicken,
          sizzling in the oven.

Matthew Roe (8)
Dalton Listerdale J&I School

SENSES

I like the look of sweets,
          wrapped in silver wrapping.

I like the feel of flowers,
          stroking my leg.

I like the sound of hills,
          being walked on day by day.

I like the smell of wool,
          being blown in the sky.

I like the taste of birds,
          singing in the fragranced air.

Phoebe Allen (8)
Dalton Listerdale J&I School

DARKNESS

As the day falls into the hands of
Night, the moon lies over the houses.
Staircases creaking while you are snuggled
Up in bed. You can hear clocks ticking.
Church bells strike midnight.

Are you scared of the dark?

Jacques Hanson (8)
Dalton Listerdale J&I School

I LIKE

I like the look of pizza,
        asking to be eaten.
I like the feel of electric guitars,
        making rocky music.
I like the taste of trees,
        swaying in the light breeze.
I like the smell of silk,
        lying on the shelf.
I like the sound of aftershave,
        bubbling when it shakes.

Alex Jones (8)
Dalton Listerdale J&I School

SENSES

I like the look of chocolate,
       melting on the table.

I like the taste of pianos,
       drifting a fresh song through the air.

I like the smell of cotton wool,
       wafting through the atmosphere.

I like the feel of bees,
       carrying their black and yellow fluffy hair.

I like the sound of flowers,
       as they rustle together in the wind.

Ben Marshall (9)
Dalton Listerdale J&I School

ME AND MY SENSES

I like the look of dogs,
       dancing in the light green grass.

I like the feel of fur,
       blowing in the cold breezy air.

I like the taste of fragrance,
       tingling in my mouth.

I like the sound of birds,
       twitching in the high trees.

I like the smell of flowers,
       tickling my legs.

Beth Royle (8)
Dalton Listerdale J&I School

I LIKE . . .

I like the look of chocolate,
>melting on the table.

I like the feel of freshly mown grass,
>dancing in the air.

I like the taste of music,
>filling the house with laughter.

I like the smell of glitter,
>fragrancing the room.

I like the sound of silk,
>whistling its little song.

Roslyn Williams (8)
Dalton Listerdale J&I School

SENSES

I like the look of flowers,
>waving in the wind.

I like the feel of perfume,
>tickling down my chest.

I like the look of stars,
>shining in the moonlight.

I like the smell of bricks,
>glinting on the house.

I like the sound of cream,
>whistling over the tree.

Laura Fletcher (8)
Dalton Listerdale J&I School

SENSES

I like the look of flowers,
       waving in the wind.

I like the taste of fur,
       tingling down my spine.

I like the feel of birds,
       twitching little, sweet songs.

I like the smell of chocolate,
       melting on my hands.

I like the sound of lavender,
       with a light, sturdy wave.

Hannah Nixon (8)
Dalton Listerdale J&I School

MY MUMMY

My mummy is cool
My mummy is beautiful
My mummy is sweet
My mummy is bony
All wrapped in white
My mummy is a
Mummy
Goodnight.
zzz
zz
z

Yasmin Ahmad (9) & Rachael Colton (8)
Dalton Listerdale J&I School

MY HAMSTER, PINKY

My hamster Pinky is a little bit tough,
She wakes up in the morning feeling a bit gruff.
She gets her food with a big huff
And walks to her room with a big puff.

Whenever my dad says, *'Spit out that stuff,'*
She comes like she's had enough.
She steps in Dad's hands that felt like fluff,
But she never feels rough.

But she's my hamster,
Don't care if she's tough or chews gloves.
She's my hamster
And she's mine to be loved.

Thomas King (9)
Dalton Listerdale J&I School

HULLABALOO!

When is it going to snow?
I want everything to look white.
I like to see the snow glistening.
When is it going to snow?
I like to play with the fluffy snow.
I like to make round, soft snowballs.
I want to make a friendly-faced snowman.
When will I wrap up warm so I don't feel icy cold?
When is it going to snow?
I can't wait until I slide down the bumpy hills.
Oohh! I wish it would snow!

Sabah Ali (10)
Dalton Listerdale J&I School

MY FAMILY

My family are always there for me.
From when I was born up to now
And they are always there for me
They are waiting for me at home right now.
That's how they are always there for me.
My brother has started driving just for me.
When it was Christmas
I asked for a bike,
My mum and dad went to get me one.
That's how they are always there for me.
They care for me,
I care for them,
I will always be there for them too.

Megan Longden (10)
Dalton Listerdale J&I School

THE WORLD

The world is not enough!
It is a place of death and pollution.
Life fades away, people argue,
Darkness fills the air.
Wars are getting terrible,
Millions of lives are obliterated,
People become homeless.
Diseases infect the hearts of innocent lives.
We have got to end the wars,
End the darkness.
Let light be shown to the world,
Make the world enough.

Ben Rutherford (10)
Dalton Listerdale J&I School

HULLABALOO!

Eminem is the best number one all of the time,
Moby, get back in line.
What's the point in having the Brits,
When Eminem will win?

Eminem is the best number one all of the time,
Shaggy, get back in line.
At the Brits, let Eminem do your bits!

Eminem is the finest, Kylie stop whining,
Let's sing 'Without Me',
I see what you mean.

Matthew Reeves (9)
Dalton Listerdale J&I School

HULLABALOO!

I loved my small white Labrador and now she's gone.
I loved the way she would chew my slipper.
I loved the way, on a summer's day, she would pounce all over me.
Dribbling, slobbery candles of spit.
Even when she barked all night.
But it isn't the same now.
My dog's name was Pippa.
They called her after me.
The only reason why I talk about Pippa today
Is because she was the best thing that happened to me.
She loved me so much, she died for me.

Philippa Spencer (10)
Dalton Listerdale J&I School

CANDYLAND

Yes, I'm back in Candyland,
Licking lollies and playing in sherbet.
Trees made of chocolate with liquorice on the top.
How I wish it was real!
How I would love to roll in colourful, chewy jelly babies.
Maybe get drunk by drinking bottles full of wine gums.
I really wish it was real, but I will be back tomorrow.

Josh Pickford (10)
Dalton Listerdale J&I School

HULLABALOO

My family is the place for me
Welcoming at the end of a day.
They are all ready to love me
Whatever I do.
I run upstairs
They run after me.
I jump up on the bed
They tuck me up tight.
I fall to sleep.
In the morning
They are all ready for my love again.
I am always happy with them.

Aimee Carter (9)
Dalton Listerdale J&I School

MY PUP, TESS

The pet I have is Tess the best,
with floppy black ears,
her little pup paws
and sharp claws,
bounds through doors.

The pet I have is Tess the best,
she likes her toys,
barks at boys.
She is my Tess
the best!

Adam Roddis (9)
Dalton Listerdale J&I School

WILD TIGER

The green-eyed tiger prowling
Along the forest track.
Hungrily he watches,
His eyes so wide.
Never he blinks, can't afford to,
All the other animals have
Heard or seen him,
Off they run,
Off to hide.
Afraid of his power.

His fur the colour of golden
Beaches,
His teeth big and bulky.
His padded feet make no sound.
His body ready to pounce.
Keeping his ears alert for any
Movement.

Jessica Parkes (10)

Dalton Listerdale J&I School

RUGBY

The game was played
Another chance has been made
The number eight comes in
As sharp as a pin
The manager makes a sub
The fans and players can't wait to get to the pub.
A conversion goes over the post
The fans make the most
The best player had the ball
He wasn't very good at all
The game was won
It was really fun.

Joe Jarvis (9)
Dalton Listerdale J&I School

FOOTBALL

We started from the spot
So it was football on the plot
The crowd went wild
As the football went down the isle
We had a shot at the goal
But the ball hit the pole
We had a shot
It was a brilliant pot
It was one-nil to us
And two minutes for a shot
It was a throw-in from the side
But the shot went wide
The whistle went
That meant
We had won
We all shook each other's hand
And the captain took off his arm band.

Nick Whyman (10)
Dalton Listerdale J&I School

THE STORM

The wild storm rages like an angry giant,
Vicious lightning bolts through the sky,
Like fiery weapons,
As its thunderous voice rumbles and echoes furiously,
The wind shrieks noisily like an angry spirit,
Its icy raindrops grip the house as tightly as a fastened rope.
The rain beats furiously against the window,
Like a bunch of raging warriors,
Inside, the fire greets us, like a dog to his master
And we feel as warm and snug,
As a cat curled up in bed.

Katie Palethorpe & Jemma Graves (11)
Dalton Listerdale J&I School

CRAZY ANIMALS

I was once in a zoo
And I saw a kangaroo.
It was hopping like mad,
Because it was so glad
And I thought to myself,
What a load of 'hullabaloo'.

I was once in a park
And I saw a funny shark.
It said, 'Hip hip hooray,
What a fine day,'
And I thought to myself,
What a load of 'hullabaloo'.

I was once at the fair
And I saw a great hare.
It was dancing along,
To the beat of a song
And I thought to myself,
What a load of 'hullabaloo'.

I was once in Hull
And I saw a fierce bull.
It was looking at the moon
And was whistling a tune
And I thought to myself,
What a load of 'hullabaloo'.

Aren't these animals a load of *'hullabaloo'?*

Grace Binnie (11) & Georgina Reynolds (10)
Dalton Listerdale J&I School

PHEASANTS

I went to the woods
With my daddy and Uncle Paul,
It was full of mud,
Had to be careful not to fall.

I had an important job
And I had to do it well,
Even though I didn't get paid a bob,
I enjoyed it, it was swell.

My job was counting shots,
Bang! Bang! The guns went,
Those poor pheasants would end up in pots,
Away the dogs went,
We bagged the pheasants,
What lovely presents!

Laura Clewes (10)
Dalton Listerdale J&I School

THE OLD HOUSE

The old house moans in the dark, cold night,
As the roof sleeps silently on top of it,
The windows chatter away
And the doors dance below.

The letter boxes gossip to each other,
As the lights glare at the spitting fire,
The hall echoes and the vibration comes squealing back,
Making the stairs twirl vigorously to the top.

Joshua Turner (11) & Christopher Bentley (10)
Dalton Listerdale J&I School

MY FAMILY

My name is Rebecca,
I'm a happy fellow,
I have blonde hair
And hazel-brown eyes.

I have a mum,
Who's as sweet as a plum,
The house is sparkling,
With all her spring cleaning.

I have a dad,
Who always gets mad,
But inside he's the best,
With his big bald head.

I have a brother,
Whose name is Stuart,
His birthday is September,
Not November, October or December.

My family, my family,
Are the best, the best
I love my family,
My funny family.

Rebecca Turner (10)
Dalton Listerdale J&I School

THE OLD HOUSE

The houses huddled together
As the roof slept lazily, while busy people pass by.
The windows chatter noisily as
The doors danced
To the rhythm of the wind.

The letter box snapped with nastiness,
While the hall stared gormlessly
The stairs twirl like a ballerina, while the lights
Beamed happily.

Emily Sanderson (10) & Jessica Royle (11)
Dalton Listerdale J&I School

THE MYSTERIOUS WOOD

The night howled
As the wind whistled through
The whispering trees.

The branches snapped at
The squealing leaves
That fell to the ground.

The man on the moon laughed
Watching the red eyes of the bushes twinkle
As the grass shuffled and shivered

The night howled
As the wind whistled through
The whispering trees.

Charlotte Collins (10) & Rachael Johnson (11)
Dalton Listerdale J&I School

PARADISE ISLAND

The pink and gold sunset in the sky
Watches fluffy white clouds passing by
Waves are lapping at the shore
On Paradise Island once more

Palm trees are ruffled with a soft breeze
So I lay back and watch with ease
Dolphins gracefully jumping in the sea
On a Paradise Island just for me

Gold sand covering the ground
As sadly morning comes around
My Paradise Island fades out of sight
It only exists in the middle of the night.

Hayley Graham (10)
Dalton Listerdale J&I School

SCARY NIGHTS

'Time for bed,'
My mother said.
I said, 'Oh no,'
For I knew the dreams I would dread.
Ghosties and ghouls and mummies all jumped out on me.
My heart beat as fast as it could be.
I tried to run as fast as I could,
But I could not move,
So I had to stay in the dream.

Rosie Davies (8)
Darton Primary School

MY MUM'S PREGNANT

My mum's pregnant,
She really really is,
I think she's going to pop then fizz.
I don't believe it,
Nor do my friends at school,
But now that she's pregnant
There's nothing to stop her now
And I hope when it's older
It'll be as cool as me.

Now that I'm at high school
My boyfriend and I
Go out together,
So I'm usually not at home.
I've never had detention,
Nor Josh (my boyfriend).
He's taking me out for tea,
I won't be here on Monday.
My mum will be lonely,
I'll come back at midnight when everyone's in bed.

Today is Sunday, tomorrow I'll be out.
I don't have to hear my big sis cry and shout.
She only cries when I'm around,
But I'll be gone,
I'm right not wrong.
Now it's night-time,
Good night . . .

All through the night I hear screams and shouts,
In comes Dad, he shakes me really hard,
'Come and see Thomas.'
As cute as cute can be
My baby brother.
I want this to happen,
Because it's not true.

Bethany Louise Blewitt (8)
Darton Primary School

FOOD

Food is brilliant,
Food is fun,
Food is for everyone.
Food is scrummy,
Food is funny,
Food is for my tummy.
Food is for eating,
Eat, eat, eat.
Food is for breakfast,
Food is for dinner,
Food is for tea,
So why don't you
Eat, eat, eat.

Lyndsey Grosse (9)
Darton Primary School

FRIENDS

Friends, friends everywhere.
Friends there to share.
Friends, friends everywhere.
Friends to love and care.

Friends, friends everywhere.
Friends to come and play.
Friends, friends everywhere.
I'd like them to stay.

William Daws (7)
Darton Primary School

HAPPY BIRTHDAY

Everybody is giving presents to me
But it is nearly ready for tea.

We play up and down till we are asleep
I will just take a peep

It is time to have the cake
We all made it, but our mums helped us.

'Whooo!' candles are out,
Pitch-black.
Then the cleaners clean up
With their sacks.

Sarah Richardson (8)
Darton Primary School

FOOTBALL CRAZY

Saturday's here
The crowd all cheer
Leeds score
We all want more

The atmosphere is great
I'm sat next to my mate
The ball is in the net
I didn't expect another one yet

Happy faces all around
No one wants to leave the ground
The whistle sounds
The match is done
Next Saturday will be fun.

Gregory Taylor (9)
Darton Primary School

THE SKY

The sky is bright,
It's snowing tonight.
Snowmen and snowballs,
Sledging is fun,
Hot chocolate and muffins
When the fun is done.

Matthew Linford (9)
Darton Primary School

TOO LATE!

The football net was open
The striker began to run
He was thinking about scoring
When the final whistle blew.

Ben Wood (9)
Darton Primary School

CATS AND DOGS

Cats and dogs are very very neat,
They think they are so sweet, sweet, sweet,
Dogs are rough and cats are weak.
My best friend has five or six,
They are very naughty and like to play tricks,
She doesn't care cos she loves them to bits,
They go to the park and chase after sticks.

Cloe Marie Lazzarano (8)
Darton Primary School

MY SPECIAL DAY

I love the Wednesday nights,
When I go to computer club,
I have my tuna sandwiches,
With a lovely fishy taste.
I like it when I listen to the birds
Singing in the evening,
I have a soothing hot bath,
Then before bed I read my favourite book,
A lovely Wednesday night.

Talia Jade Sheekey (8)
Darton Primary School

FLOWERS

A tulip is red,
Red like a love heart.

A sunflower is yellow,
With orange in the middle.

A daffodil is yellow all over.

Violets are blue,
Light blue or dark blue.

Fern Bowes (7)
Darton Primary School

ROCKY THE ROCK STAR

Rocky the rock star
Was a pop star.
He was always on TV,
He made so many records,
He was a big celebrity.

James Cooke (9)
Darton Primary School

FOOTBALL CRAZY

I'm football crazy,
I'm football mad,
I'm football crazy
And so is my dad.
We watch it on a Saturday,
We watch it on TV,
We are the greatest supporters
Of the team NUFC.

Joe Fletcher (8)
Darton Primary School

DOGS

Charles spaniels sniffing the air,
Labradors running about all day.
Dogs barking all day long and that's what they do best.
Boxers tugging your socks as they go to play.
Golden retrievers eating all day.
Basset hounds' ears dangling all day.
Dogs with soft and hard fur,
But I don't care if they are soft or hard
Because I like them all.

Makayla Megan England (8)
Darton Primary School

DOLPHINS

Dolphins are friendly
Dolphins are nice
Dolphins are everything I dream of at night
Dolphins can swim
Dolphins can leap
I wish I had a dolphin of my very own to keep
I love dolphins.

Melanie Jade Heald (8)
Darton Primary School

LITTLE BEE

There was a bee,
Sat on a wall,
It said, *buzz buzz*
And that was all.

Matthew John Holdsworth (9)
Darton Primary School

JAMES BOND

The roads are hot
Just like the car
That's melting the tar
The car is fast
That's why you're never last!

James Ledger
Darton Primary School

A PARROT

Can a parrot eat a carrot
Standing on his head?
If it did my mum would send me
Straight up to bed.

Emma Casey (9)
Darton Primary School

BARNSLEY SWIMMING CLUB

Barnsley swimming club is so ace,
I win a trophy nearly every race.
'Well done,' that's what the coaches say
When you go for your trophy everyone shouts, 'Hooray.'
The one who loses feels so so sad,
I go up to them and say, 'Hey it's not all that bad.'
When you are training you work very hard,
Every year you receive a membership card.
Now our champion needs to be seen,
Everyone, our champion is Laura Green.

Laura Green (10)
Dearne Carrfield Primary School

MY FAMILY AND FRIENDS

My sister is pretty
My dog is bad
My cousin is noisy
My mum is mad
My grandma is wacky
My grandad is late
My dad is funny
My family are great
Winston is bossy
Ellis is shy
Jordan is funny
Sarah is sly
Zoe is quiet
Brandon is a pest
Patrick has scored a goal
My friends are the best.

Lauren Marsh (10)
Dearne Carrfield Primary School

MY FAMILY

My dad is very tall,
My mum is quite small.
My brother is crazy,
My cousin is lazy.
My auntie is fond of dogs,
My uncle collects logs.
My grandads have lost their hair,
My nanas love and care
And me: I love them all.

Emily Morris (9)
Dearne Carrfield Primary School

THE KITE THAT GOT STUCK IN THE TREE

I was flying my kite one day
And it suddenly flew away,
It had got stuck in a tree,
I needed help that was the key.

I called my dad,
He's an inch too small,
We called my mum,
She was just as tall.

Well the kite it just sat,
Like a lazy old cat,
The kite was looking rather sad,
I was getting dreadfully mad,
It swirled around
And fell to the ground.

Joshua Oskinski (8)
Dearne Carrfield Primary School

HOME AGAIN

Home again back from school,
I'm going out to play - how cool!
Time to come in for my tea,
Lots of sandwiches all for me,
I watch TV for a little while,
Have a wash and go to bed,
Fast asleep to rest my head.

Leigh Jones (9)
Dearne Carrfield Primary School

MY PLAYHOUSE

My playhouse is a brilliant place such wonderful things it has.
It's three levels high and the washing machine goes round and round,
It looks like it's going to fly.
The oven is so very hot,
It will surely scald you if you touch a pot.
The arts and crafts box has glue and paint,
The glue is sticky which I hate.
The third floor of my playhouse shed is where I keep my little bed.
Sometimes on this very high place I rest my small but sleepy head.

Brogan Hough (8)
Dearne Carrfield Primary School

WIND

Wind is weather
Wind is fast
Wind blows off people's hats.

Wind blows hard
Wind blows cold
To go out in it you have to be bold
Wind, wind, wind, wind, wind
What happens in the wind?

Barry Pugh (8)
Dearne Carrfield Primary School

HODDLY PODDLY

Hoddly poddly puddle and fogs
Cats have to marry the poodle dogs
Cats in black jackets and dogs in red hats
What will become of the mice and the rats.

Kirsty Booth (9)
Dearne Carrfield Primary School

POP

I went to the shop,
To buy some pop,
On the way I decided to hop, hop, hop.

As I got to the shop,
I heard a loud *pop!*
So I hopped into the shop, shop, shop.

The pop in the shop
Had gone *pop, pop, pop.*
So the lady gave me a mop, mop, mop.

Sarah Gauntley (9)
Dearne Carrfield Primary School

MY SISTER

My sister is not nice,
She is so annoying,
When I am asleep
She makes a bleep,
When I wake up
I play with my pup
She always comes to spoil my game
Things will never be quite the same.

Chloe Nolan (8)
Dearne Carrfield Primary School

MY PARROT

I have a parrot, he is my pal
We enjoy hearing him caw,
He twerps and tweets,
He even takes my sweets.
What a cheeky fellow
His feathers are green and yellow.

Scooby is his name
And sometimes he drives me insane.
He flies around loopy, so I call out *Scooby!*
But still he does as he please.

I like to watch him blink,
His eyes are so cute I think.
Sometimes he bites my finger,
When I do not let him linger.

His favourite thing is a lollipop stick,
Sometimes I feel he's taking the mick.
Scooby is my friend
And I will love him to the end.

Kyle Frost (8)
Dearne Carrfield Primary School

FRUIT

Bananas they are yellow,
They are so good to eat.
Sometimes I have them for breakfast
Because they are so sweet.

I also like apples,
I have one every day,
Because they keep you healthy
They keep the doctor away.

We all like our fruit,
We should have five a day.
It is supposed to keep our strength up
At work, at rest, at play.

James Chambers (9)
Dearne Carrfield Primary School

MY HORSE

I ride a horse
She rides through a course
My horse like carrots
But doesn't like parrots
My daddy doesn't like her
Because he is a stinker
She's lots of fun
She can run
She can jump as high as a jump
She can jump over a bump
She's called Ellie and
Has a big belly
She is my friend.

Charlotte Arundell (8)
Dearne Carrfield Primary School

COLOURS

C   is for colours all over the world
O   is for orange so sweet like sugar
L   is for laces as long as snakes
O   is for oink the pig is very noisy
U   is for umbrella it's raining very fast
R   is for rainbow yahoo!

Sophie Thompson (7)
Dearne Carrfield Primary School

HOME AGAIN

Home again after a day at school,
First it's tea . . . not just for me,
Then the bath . . . and the loo,
Time for bed to relax my head
Ready for another day at school.

Nathan Thompson (8)
Dearne Carrfield Primary School

FOOTBALL

I like football, I play for a club.
I practise on Tuesdays, it makes me feel good.
Although it is tiring I give it my all.

I run and tackle till I win the ball.
I pass the ball and soon get it back.
I pull back my foot and give it a crack.
It goes through the air like a bullet in flight.
It goes in the net to my delight.

A few seconds left till full-time.
As the whistle blows the glory is mine.
The players come to give me a hug.
Everyone said that I played really good.

It's Tuesday again back to training I go.
In the next match see if I can repeat the show.

Aiden Cooper (9)
Dearne Carrfield Primary School

MY KITE

I was flying my kite,
When it was light,
Then it turned to a dark, dark night
And then my kite went out of sigh.
When it was light,
The sun shone bright,
I saw my kite at such a height.
Then when it came dark,
There was only a spark.

Rebecca Stocks (8)
Dearne Carrfield Primary School

MY MUM

My mum is wicked,
She takes the Mickey out of me
She's sometimes gormless
Sometimes thick
And sometimes tickle me
Until I am nearly sick.
She cooks my meals
And irons my clothes
She even washes between my toes
I sometimes make her mad,
I sometimes make her glad,
I sometimes take her chewing gum out of her bag.
The one thing I would like to say
Or even shout out loud
Is she's the best mum in the world
And I love her without a doubt.

Eden Shortt (8)
Dearne Carrfield Primary School

MY DOG CASSIE

I've got a little puppy
Her name is called Cassie
She's such a cute lassie
My Cassie is a black Labrador
And she follows me to the door.
She likes her breakfast, dinner and tea
And she likes to follow me.
She is seven weeks old
And doesn't like to go out in the cold.
She's my little puppy
And I love her very much.

Janina Sills (8)
Dearne Carrfield Primary School

MY DOG MERLIN

My dog sleeps like a log,
He never moves a bit,
Every time he scratches,
We think it is a nit,
Ever since I saw him,
I had wishes from the heart,
That he would be as special,
As he was right from the start.

Jordan Ratcliffe (9)
Dearne Carrfield Primary School

MY WORLD

Right is wrong, wrong is right.
Night is day and day is night.

Yes is no, no is yes,
But no one takes any interest.

With this letter that I send,
I hope you understand.

If you want to know the name,
You have to read this poem again.

Vanessa Minshull (8)
Dearne Carrfield Primary School

MY FRIENDS

I've got two friends called Jenny and Penny
They think they're good but they're not so funny
They break my toys and what a noise,
My two friends Jenny and Penny,
They are pains but what a shame,
They tickle my dog when he is on the bog,
My two friends called Jenny and Penny.

Ellie McCrystal (8)
Dearne Carrfield Primary School

MY CHOCOLATE CAR

I wish I had a chocolate car,
To drive to the highest star,
With headlamps made of Smarties,
We'd go to all the parties.
The seats made of marshmallow,
Their colour would be yellow.
The steering wheel,
A Wagon Wheel,
Petrol made of cream,
We'd go so fast I'd scream,
We'd drive around at night
And be home by first light.

Joshua Marsh (8)
Dearne Carrfield Primary School

MY FAT CAT

My fat cat doesn't move from her mat,
Doesn't move from her mat all day.
She lies on her mat, the big, fat cat,
No matter what we say.

When it was wet we sent for the vet
Who came in a Ford Fiesta,
He seemed in a hurry, and said,
'Don't worry, she's just in a long siesta.'

Charlie Ludlam (8)
Dearne Carrfield Primary School

MIKEY THE HEDGEHOG

I'm small and I'm spikey
My name is Mikey.
I scurry and worry
I'm always in a hurry.
My bed is a bunk
In an old tree trunk.
I'm a little scared, but
I'm friendly too.
If you put out a little food
I may come to you.
I might come tonight
If that's alright,
Or tomorrow, when it's light.

Jasmine Hopper (9)
Dearne Carrfield Primary School

MY TEDDY

My teddy is cute and fluffy,
I decided to call her Muffy.
She is a cat with a little pink nose,
I think she smells just like a rose.
With her white body and pink ears,
She cheers me up when I'm in tears.
My teddy is cute and fluffy
And her name is Muffy.

Katrina Pugh (9)
Dearne Carrfield Primary School

I'M AN ALIEN

I'm an alien creature from out of space,
With an alien body and an alien face.
I've got sixty-four alien toes
And an extra terrestrial purple nose
Alien creatures have alien arms
And they count them all with physical charms
Bright green ears and luminous eyes,
Golly, I'm a good looking guy.

Jasmine Hall (10)
Dearne Carrfield Primary School

SKATEBOARDING

There's a man called Freddy,
He's on the line ready
For his big course.
There he goes faster and faster,
He will end up with his foot in plaster!
He's daring, he's clever and he cares nothing for the weather.
Bashing and crashing,
Jumping and bumping,
Turning and swerving,
Grinding and colliding,
The ladies are scared,
Because they care.
There he goes over a ramp up in the air as far as he can,
Then he's grinding on a frame of a van.
Riding and gliding,
Flipping and gripping,
Stalling and falling,
Speeding and weaving.
There he goes the Skateboard King,
You can hear the crowd sing.
Now he is coming to the end of his trials,
The crowd are giving him lots of smiles.
They are clapping loud
And Freddy is proud.
It is the end of the day,
His memories will stay.

Brandon Crook & Patrick Desbrough (10)
Dearne Carrfield Primary School

MY FAMILY

Mum

My mum has got a caring heart,
She's always trying to do her part.
Whenever I've been really bad,
She's never ever really mad.

Dad

My dad is a computer freak,
Sometimes people call him a geek.
He likes his cars,
Likes some people like iron bars.
That's my dad you see.

Donna

Donna is my sister she's always trying to wind me up,
When we have coffee she drinks from a cup.
She works all day
And comes home to play.
She's the friendly one every day.

Pagan

Pagan is my dog,
She likes chewing logs.
She can be really funny,
Once she tried to chew my money.

Jordan Clark (10)
Dearne Carrfield Primary School

WAR

Why do we have to start a fight?
Can't there be a law?
People go to fight
I'd hate to see the sight
What would happen to us all?
One bomb that could kill us all.

Cody Mellor (9)
Dearne Carrfield Primary School

DOGS, DOGS . . .

Dogs, dogs
What a pest
Chewing up slippers
Making a mess
Dogs, dogs
Mine's a pest
But I love her
She's the best.

Katie Jackson (9)
Dearne Carrfield Primary School

CHOCOLATE LAND

C hocolate Land! Chocolate Land!
H ow many chocolates?
O ne, two, three, four is there any more?
C hocolate land! Chocolate Land!
O h Chocolate Land!
L ovely Chocolate Land,
A ll the chocolate in the land is lovely,
T rees with milk or white chocolate Land
E ven trees with Smarties

L ovely Chocolate Land,
A ll the lollipops are lovely
N o boys allowed in Chocolate Land!
D o you want to visit Chocolate Land?

Rebecca Orton (10)
Dearne Carrfield Primary School

THE PEOPLE I KNOW

My mum is kind and sweet.
My dad just loves to eat.
My brother drives me round the bend,
But Jordan is my very best friend.
My sister likes to play on her phone,
Lauren just likes to moan.
But most of all what's best for me,
Is staying at Grandma's for my tea.

Sarah Cavell (10)
Dearne Carrfield Primary School

THINGS I LOVE

The smell of my mum's perfume,
As she kisses me goodnight.

The sound of the sea,
As it crashes against the rocks.

The vibration of the plane,
As we fly off to Tenerife.

The sound of laughter,
As we're playing on the beach.

The softness of my bed,
As I slide into the sheets.

The sound of the bowling ball,
As it rolls down the alley.

Rachel Boam (11)
Ferham Primary School

THE NIGHT SKY

A giant sheet of darkness,
Lit up by a silvery moon,
She wraps me in her kind cloak of darkness,
Her misty eyes look down at her world,
She guides a small shower of glittering stars across the sky,
The moon and stars rise and set, at one flick of her cloak,
She wears a slender black robe,
Cold,
She scares the Earth with her icy cloak
And when the day is over she hides away the sun.

Frances Hughes (10)
Greystones Primary School

THE BIRTHDAY

The birthday boy is walking down the street,
He looks down at the ground,
Oh my, oh my, whose are those great big feet?
'They're mine! They're mine!' says a voice from behind,
'They're so, so big don't you think?'
'Oh yes, they are a bit too big,
Well, at least they are mine, not yours
Don't you think?'

Angela Walker (9)
Holy Rood RC Primary School

HULLABALOO

I have a little hamster, Hermione is her
name . . .
She used to be rather wild, now she's quite
tame . . .
She spins around in her wheel late at
night . . .
Sometimes she gives my sister a dreadful
fright . . . !

Hannah Gregson (9)
Holy Rood RC Primary School

MY BEST FRIENDS

My friends are very fine
We are an unbreakable group of nine!
We all know how to have fun
Any kind of weather, rain or sun!
I couldn't live without my friends
Here my poem nearly ends
Even if sometimes we can fight
Not to worry we make things right,
On my friends, my friends,
My life depends
I don't have a best friend
That's fine,
I have nine!

Rebecca Wilkin (9)
Holy Rood School RC Primary School

THE TURTLE

There was a little turtle
He lived in a box
He swam in a puddle
He climbed up the rocks
He snapped at a mosquito
He snapped at a flea
He snapped at a minnow
He snapped at me.

Thomas Keating (9)
Holy Rood RC Primary School

ALPHABET POEM

My mates

A is for Amelia
Who is a very kind girl
B is for Brett
Who is sometimes very bored
C is for Chloe
Who always wears pink
D is for Delia
Who dives in puddles
E is for Elizabeth
Who often potty
F is for Freddy
Who is also very nutty
G is for Georgia
Who drives me up the wall
H is for Hollie
The craziest girl.

Chantelle Beet (9)
Hoyland Common Primary School

A FUNNY NAME POEM

A is for Andrea who likes to walk
B is for Bethany who likes to talk
C is for Carol who likes to travel
D is for Dad who likes to moan
E is for Ellie who finished a puzzle
F is for Fred who likes to eat bread
G is for George who watches tele
H is for Harry who's always in a hurry
I is for Ian who likes to scurry
J is for Joseph who chases girls
K is for Kath who's got loads of curls
L is for Liam who's got a lolly.

Tamsin O'Brien (9)
Hoyland Common Primary School

ALPHABET POEM

A is for Amelia
Who finished her work,
B is for Bethany
Who sits very nice,
C is for Chantelle
Who eats ice,
D is Dad
Who sits around,
E is for Ellie
Whose sister is Lauren,
F is for Fred
Who jumps around,
G is for Gran
Who is nutty,
H is for Holly
Whose cousin is Bethany.

Bethany O'Brien (9)
Hoyland Common Primary School

MY DOGS

Their grey fur
The small black eyes
Also the ears that flop to the side
They yap! And bark! And moan tonight.
Scurry and hurry in the grass -
Looking like deer and meant to bite.
Sleeping peacefully in the night.
Snoring loudly tonight
But one more thing,
I'll love them forever.
    Good night, sleep tight.

Lorna Welch (8)
Hoyland Common Primary School

ALPHABET POEM

A is for apple
Which falls from a tree.
B is for beetroot
As red as can be.
C is for candles
On top of a cake.
D is for doughnuts
To eat with a shake.
E is for eagle
That soars in the sky.
F is for farm
Where you see pigs in a sty.
G is for garden
With colours so bright.
H is for headlights
That shine in the night.
I is for ice cream
I eat when it's hot.
J is for jam
That you get from a pot.
K is for ketchup
You eat on your chips.
L is for licking
You do to your lips.
M is for monkey
You see in the zoo.
N is for nougat
A sweet you can chew.
O is for octopus
That lives in the sea.
P is for pasta
I like for my tea.
Q is for quilt
All warm on my bed.
R is for
My favourite colour red.

S is for summer
The time I like most.
T is for toaster
I use to make toast.
U is for umbrella
To keep me dry.
V is for vampires
That fly in the sky.
W is for water
You have in a lake.
X is for X-ray
A doctor can take.
Y is for yellow
The colour of sun.
Z is for zoo
We visit for fun.

Brett Jubb (9)
Hoyland Common Primary School

MY KITTEN

My kitten runs like mad
And he sometimes makes me mad
He runs like lightning
But to dogs he's sometimes frightening.

He's tough
He's rough
He's dangerous
He's creepy
But to me he's my friend.

Alex Owen (9)
Hoyland Common Primary School

THE NUMBER POEM

One is for the sun that shone
Two might mean you've caught the flu
Three your dog's got the flea
Number four don't forget to open the door
Number five stay alive
Number six get me that Twix
Number seven yes you've gone to Heaven
Number eight you've got into a bit of a fight
Number nine I'm fine
Number ten start all over again.

Joe Greenhough (8)
Hoyland Common Primary School

THE NAME POEM

A if for Angela who eats lots of sweets
B is for Bethany who's kind and sweet
C is for Carly who's not so sweet
D is for Dudley who eats dirty sweets
E is for Elizabeth who chases all the boys
F is for Fred who eats all the bread
G is for George who watches TV
H is for Harry who thinks he has wings.

Joseph Platts (8)
Hoyland Common Primary School

VALENTINE'S DAY

Valentine's Day, Valentine's Day
Valentine's Day is for you
Please be my valentine
Or I will kiss you
Valentine's Day, Valentine's Day
Valentine's Day is for me
If you don't want to be mine
Then don't change your mind.

Jake Adams (8)
Hoyland Common Primary School

AN ALPHABET POEM

A is for Amy
Who is a girl

B is for Beth
Who has curls

C is for Carly
Who paints her toes

D is for Danny
Who has lots of toys

E is for Elizabeth
Who is mad

F is for Fred
Who is bad

G is for Geraldine
Who is fat

H is for Hilda
Who is a cat

I is for Isabel
Who meets a bear

J is for Jade
Who likes to dare

K is for Kinsley
Who gets in muddles

L is for Liam
Who sleeps in puddles

M is for Mary
Who wets the bed
N is for Nathan
Who likes his ted

O is for Olivia

Who likes bikes

P is for Paul
Who likes hikes

Q is for Quinney
Who is running

R is for Ryan
Who likes pudding

S is for Sara
Who likes trains

T is for Terri
Who is a pain

U is for Una
Who is a dog

V is for Volar
Who likes hogs

X is for Xshanda
Who likes toys

Y is for Yvonne
Who likes paints

Z is for Zina
Who always faints.

Laura Wood (9)
Hoyland Common Primary School

GRIEF

Dying pains drumming on my bones,
Loved ones now perished,
Life isn't the same,
Lonely like the moon,
Unhealing wounds,
Wolf teeth sink into my burning heart,
Overloaded with tears,
Unspeakable pains,
Black clouds linger,
Dyed into the silence of the night . . .

Kimberley Sayles (10)
Hoyland Common Primary School

HAPPINESS

Sunny days on the beach
I wish they'd never end
The blue sky
With its fluffy clouds
Flying above me
I see the children
Playing their little games
As I feel I want to join them.
Let the dolphin of happiness
Free from its tank.

Elisabeth Platts (9)
Hoyland Common Primary School

SADNESS

Locked inside a world of tears,
Endless nights of darkness,
Curled up in a corner,
Hiding from my fear.

Deep, empty holes in my body,
That can never be refilled,
All the happiness in my life
Has slowly disappeared.

Sophie Adderley (10)
Hoyland Common Primary School

LONELINESS

Tears dripping down my cheeks,
The voice of loneliness speaks
Anger and sadness grow stronger.

Lonely like and a head with no brain
And like being tied up by a chain
Sometimes loneliness hits me
Like a punch in the stomach.

Tyler Vaines (9)
Hoyland Common Primary School

LONELINESS

As I walked down the corridor of loneliness,
A splinter of emptiness stabbed into me,
My soul was sticking to loneliness
Like a spider sticking to its web.

As I walked further down the corridor
I started to drown further in the darkness
Like a ship drowning in the sea,
The waves washed me away from my friends.

I was uncomfortably locked out of the world,
I heard the keys lock the cage door,
I turned round and saw the weeping whale,
With each tear making a puddle of emptiness.

Liam Birks (10)
Hoyland Common Primary School

REVENGE

Rage, revenge
Stamping feet
Flames, fire
Grinding teeth
Anger swelling
Brain erupting,
Eyes popping . . .
Revenge is sweet.

Sam Westerman (10)
Hoyland Common Primary School

LONELINESS

I see gloom all around,
I stare at the moonlit ground,
As I drift in the lonely sea
I think who's going to come to me,
A world of emptiness fills my head
'Just look at the people inside,' I said,
All comfortable next to the fire
Ready to go to bed
And I'm out here all alone,
Alone in this shed.

Melissa Erwin (9)
Hoyland Common Primary School

LONELINESS

As she sits in the basket and bin,
Drifting in a sea of loneliness
Reading a book with no pictures
She has a mind with no thoughts.

Loneliness sinks into her heart and head
As happiness dies away.
She feels grumpiness and nastiness
Scream in her face.

She wishes it would go away.

Siobhan Ritchie (10)
Hoyland Common Primary School

GRIEF

Ripped apart
Deadly surprise
Weak
Graveyard
Time had stopped
Destruction of life
Powerless to come back
Robbed
Tears slid across my eyes
A vibration of sadness on my bones
Black screamed across my face
My thoughts had been shattered
No point living anymore.

John Werboweckjy (11)
Hoyland Common Primary School

RED ANGER

Red is anger punching you in the face,
Red is lava in my heart,
Red is a vein bursting all day,
Red is a charging rhino,
Red is anger blinding my eyes,
Red is a cloud of anger coming over me,
Red is hot like an erupting volcano,
Red is a hot dagger slashing my heart,
Red is like fire burning my soul,
Red is the devil in the sky.

Ashley Burkinshaw (10)
Hoyland Common Primary School

LONELINESS

Overrun by loneliness,
Unknown by a crowd,
Trapped in a cage of sadness,
Just about to die,
Waking up to darkness,
Hollow heart of fire,
Drowning in a pool of loneliness,
Stranded in empty streets,
Feeling of happiness,
Stranded in desolate fields of sorrow.

Matthew Smith (10)
Hoyland Common Primary School

ANGER

Anger is red
Anger glows like smouldering ashes
Anger explodes like a bomb
Anger strikes like an angry lion
Anger is like a raging red rhino
Anger is a bloodthirsty animal
Devil cries of bloodthirsty anger
Anger is like fire burning my soul
Anger is like a punch in your face
Anger is like rage pouring out of my veins.

David Longford (10)
Hoyland Common Primary School

ANGER

Angry storms rising higher
As I toss on a sea of rage.
Nothing but noxious waves
Splash against my face.
As my aching body
Starts to fill with anger.
I grit my teeth and tighten my fists
And scream like a raging bull.

Corey Sadler-Knott (10)
Hoyland Common Primary School

LONELINESS

I stand alone in the playground,
No one is there to help me,
As the loneliness swallows me whole,
I cry tears of loneliness,
Because I'm alone in the crowd.

The silence is deafening,
I cry out,
But no sound reaches my ears,
I feel like a book without any pages,
Or a window without any glass.

My fingers are ice-blue,
I am trapped,
Trapped in a cage of loneliness,
Then a bell rings
And I am set free.

Sarah Hirst (11)
Hoyland Common Primary School

LONELINESS

Clouds start to lower as the loneliness surrounds me,
My soul sticking to loneliness like a spider to its web.

Frosty tears rolled down my solitude cheeks
As I curled into the empty corner,
A splinter of loneliness stabbed into me like a knife into butter.

Looked away from the world by a huge gate of loneliness,
My hollow heart broken in two halves.

The feel of the years 1914 and 1939 happening again,
My soul screaming to break free,
I feel as lonely as can be!

Tanya Robinson (10)
Hoyland Common Primary School

MY DAD WAS BLOWING UP

My dad was blowing up
His cheeks were red traffic lights
The sofa was like a battlefield
And the kitchen was a knocked over dustbin.

My dad was blowing up
His veins were bursting in his neck
His teeth were gritted like iron bars
And his crunching bones made me shiver.

My dad was blowing up
He used me as a punchbag
And my brother as a crash dummy
But last of all he used my mummy
As a sandwich.

Lindsey Whitmore (10)
Hoyland Common Primary School

ANGER

Red is anger
Red is lava in my veins
Red is anger in my eyes
Red is pain in my heart
Red is a raging rhino
Red is like a vein popping
Red is fire in my soul
Red is a devil in the clouds
Red is a bloodthirsty animal
Red is a snarl of a lion
Red is acid on my tongue
Red is like ripping off the roof.

Jonathan Owen (11)
Hoyland Common Primary School

LONELINESS

Stranded on your own island of loneliness
With no one there to comfort you.
It's like sitting there behind bars with loneliness,
Everybody is in the island of happiness . . . but you.
Walking into a cave of loneliness,
With jealousy right beside you.
A storm of loneliness, a river of sadness,
Fear sticking to you like superglue.

Sheridan Griffiths (10)
Hoyland Common Primary School

LONELINESS

Clouds start to lower
as loneliness surrounds me,
It spreads into my body
through my broken heart.

As a splinter was stabbed into me
like a knife into butter,
My soul was sticking to the room
like a spider to a web.

Rhiannon Sharp (9)
Hoyland Common Primary School

I SMASHED THE BATHROOM WINDOW

The fury on Dad's face,
My mum was stood as if her mind was up in space,
My dad screamed, 'Who's gonna pay that window bill?'
I sat in the corner saying, 'I will, I will.'
Thunder and lightning argue over the top of my dad's head,
As Mum came down from space and sent me up to bed.

Kelsey Green (10)
Hoyland Common Primary School

MONKEY

'Monkey, monkey, wait for me
because I want to climb with you.'
'Monkey, monkey what are you doing?'
'I'm swinging on a tree.'
'No you're not, you're falling in the sea.'
Splash, spash! A dolphin zoomed like a car
it flipped him on his back
'Monkey, are you OK?'
'Yes, I'm OK, just a little pain in my back.'

Jamie Gardner (9)
Hoyland Common Primary School

DOLPHIN

'Dolphin, dolphin what you going to do?'
'I'm coming to swim with you.'
'Dolphin, dolphin what you going to do?'
'I'm coming to find some shells with you.'
'You'd better get swimming
I'm coming to catch you
A, B, C, 1, 2, 3
Here I come!'

Amy Bramley (9)
Hoyland Common Primary School

THE LION

Lion, lion of the night,
Creeps around in the night,
When the lights come out
He hides and shouts,
Go away sunlight.

Lion, lion of the night,
Your teeth are like a needle,
Your knees are hairy
And your face is furry.

Lion, lion in the night,
What are you doing?
I am going to eat a postman.

Bridie Mayock (8)
Hoyland Common Primary School

THE DOLPHIN

Dolphin, dolphin, what you going to do?
I'm coming in the sea with you.
I'm coming on your back
You better jump because I'm coming
In the sea with you.
Dolphin you're blue, you're fat
And I'm coming in the sea with you.
Dolphin, dolphin, what you going to do?
I'm coming to sleep with you,
I'm coming to sleep with you!

Eden Turner (8)
Hoyland Common Primary School

JEALOUSY

Jealousy germs surround me
In every direction I go
As the disease spreads
And the poisonous snake of jealousy
Digs its teeth into me
Harder and harder
I begin to think of ways
To hurt other people
The envy volcano has boiled
And rushed everywhere.

Rebekkah Loczki (9)
Hoyland Common Primary School

ANGER

Anger is black, dark blue and purple,
You will fall down in darkness.
It will feel like fire burning like the sun in your head,
It will sound like witches killing you in your nightmares.
The lightning will hit you like a bright flashlight,
The thunder will rip through the sky like rage.

Katie Cross (10)
Hoyland Common Primary School

FEAR

As the sun finally lays its golden head
The cold fingers of fear creep out from their hiding place
They tightened their grip on my arm
And pulled me into a deep, dark pit of fear
As the blanket of darkness surrounds
I reach for the light switch but cannot find it
The blanket of darkness smothers me
I fall into a pit of darkness
And watch the sheep of sleep stroll by.

Ryan Burdin (9)
Hoyland Common Primary School

HAPPINESS

Summer shining bright
Orange, red and yellow,
Holidays that never end,
Full of sunny weather,
Laughter fills the air,
Like the oxygen I breathe,
Someone walked along the beach,
I looked up. Spencer!

Katie Derbyshire (11)
Hoyland Common Primary School

SADNESS

Endless nights of tears locked inside my heart
Lonely as it feels in a pool of dark
Curled up in fright, deep in my eyes
All the nights of freedom has gone from my life
All my friends have disappeared into the night sky
Now it's time to say goodbye.

Charlotte Aimee Robinson (10)
Hoyland Common Primary School

THE VOLCANO

As hot fire booms out of
His hollow, echoing voice,
His scorching breath is full
Of poisonous gas and his
Bloodshot eyes go even gloomier.
Hot, bulging fire erupts from his
Scorching, fierce teeth.
He spits lava at me and snaps his
Jaws repeatedly, as I try to make
My way past him.
He flows even faster, I start to
Panic, as I try to escape my feet
Start to shake.
But after all it was just my dad
Yelling at me.

Nicola Davies (10)
Hoyland Common Primary School

THE VOLCANO

The giant beast roars in anger,
screaming and shouting, his voice echoing.
The beast wants more blood
devouring people, horror, pain and death.
The bloodthirsty beast suffocating his prey.
Scorching breath like poisonous gas.
The beast spits lava at people
melting them to ash.
Fiery-red burning hair, bloodshot eyes,
people screaming, the beast slavers lava
before he's knocked out, sleeping.
Who knows when the beast will explode again?

Luke Micklethwaite (10)
Hoyland Common Primary School

VOLCANO

The volcano is dormant, waiting for its time.
The volcano is a devil,
Its breath scorching like poisonous gas.
Its voice booms and echoes
It spews ash, dust and lava
It's like a devil.
Piercing, glooming, glowing and beaming eyes.
Devils lurk in its eyes,
The volcano eyes bring death and destruction.
The volcano's hair burning, sizzling, red, matted.
Hair like fire, bringing doom.
You can't hide from its destruction.
Its voice deep, booming echoes in the air.
Its hollow, fierce voice will scare you
And make you run as fast as you can.
The volcano is a giant with a long, bushy beard
Killing millions with just a touch.
Fists of anger spitting at people.
He is tall and brings a stream of pain with its anger.
It is now lying dormant.
It does not wake till the next time
It will bring more destruction.

Elliott Parker (10)
Hoyland Common Primary School

MISS BATTERSBY'S CLASS

M y teacher is beautiful and lovely
I like school because I like writing.
S ome people are nice
S ome people are bad

B oys mess around sometimes
A t school I play with my friends
T eachers are good all the time
T eachers are helpful and kind
E llie is my best friend
R ead the book I read
S ing with me tomorrow
B e my best friend
Y our birthday is on the 9th of May.
S ee me at the spider's web

C an you come to my house?
L aura is kind to me.
A my is my best friend too
S ee me at the seaside
S chool councils are really good.

Lauren Cross (7)
Hoyland Common Primary School

COLOUR POEM

Yellow is a bright colour like the sun.
Green is a lovely colour for the grass.
Blue is the best colour for the sky.
Red is a very nice colour for the bright sunset.
Pink is a very subtle colour for a princess' dress.
Brown is a lovely colour for a horse.
White is a wonderful colour for milk to drink.
Gold is a good colour for a princess' make-up.
Silver is a suitable colour for a car.
Grey is a great colour for an elephant.
Orange is a good colour for an orange.
Dark blue is a nice colour for a school shirt.
Dark green is a nice colour for a school jumper.

Jessica Mellars (7)
Hoyland Common Primary School

MISS BATTERSBY

M y teacher is fantastic
I   like school
S   ome boys mess
S   ome boys don't mess

B   oys are awfully rude, well some
A   t half-past three we all go home.
T   ime for dinner at twelve o'clock
T   eachers always help whatever you're doing
E   arly start to the day
R   ummaging through books trying to find one to read
S   tocking up books that I knocked over
B   oys are sometimes sweet
Y   ou always behave for every teacher.

Amy Louise Rooney (8)
Hoyland Common Primary School

THE WEATHER

Weather, weather will you change?
I'm fed up of you, you're driving me insane
Come out sun, leave the rain behind
But I'd rather be in Spain out of the rain.

Jacob Bellamy (7)
Hoyland Common Primary School

BLUE

Blue is like the ocean crashing on the rocks
Blue is the sky on a very calm night
Blue is like the dolphins, dipping and diving
Blue is like water, dripping in a pot
Drip, drop, drip, drop, everywhere I stop.

Samantha Sidebottom (8)
Hoyland Common Primary School

MY TEACHER'S CREATURE

My teacher had a big creature that wriggled in its cage
The children liked the creature even though it was in a rage.
My teacher had a big creature that wriggled in its cage.
They did not know what to do with it so they let it go away.

Sam Birtles (8)
Hoyland Common Primary School

COLOUR POEM

Red is like a fire
burning at night.
Yellow is like the sun
shining in the sky.
White is like the moon
shining at night.
Purple is like my pencil
which I write with.

Georgia Evans (8)
Hoyland Common Primary School

FIRE

Flaming hot, burning red
Flickers of yellow and blue
Flames that are reaching high
Right up into the sky.
It reaches up
Come back down
Now that's fire.

Brooke Green (8)
Hoyland Common Primary School

MY TEACHER POEM

My teacher Miss Battersby takes me for literacy
My teacher Miss Battersby is very nice to me
She helps me with my work when I am stuck
She sometimes lets us do fun things
She also gives us hard spellings
But then some are easy.
That is my teacher Miss Battersby
Who takes me for literacy.

Carly Hogan (8)
Hoyland Common Primary School

FOOTBALL CRAZY

Football crazy
Felt like a daisy
Had a big game
What a shame
We lost 6-0,
Because we played up hill.
It turned to hail
Thanks to Dale.
Tried to sing
But sounded like the wind.
My leg was aching
Danny was baking.

Billy Evans (7)
Hoyland Common Primary School

CATS

Cats are furry
They come in different shapes and sizes
Some are stripy, some are skinny,
Some have long tails
And some are steady,
Cats are fast runners,
Cats are lovely and cuddly and soft.

Shannon Harris (8)
Hoyland Common Primary School

CATS AND DOGS

Cats have staring eyes
that watch you at night.
They're furry and funny,
but they sometimes give you a fright.
Dogs are fat, dogs like cats,
dogs are mad, one's a lad,
dogs are light, so you can see them at night.

Bradley Thornton (7)
Hoyland Common Primary School

MY DOG

My dog is cuddly,
He is snugly
And he licks
Although he chases sticks.

My dog chews the post,
But I still love him,
He can drive Mum up the wall,
Well, he can jump up so tall.

My dog is cuddly,
He is snugly
And he licks,
But he loves me and I love him.

Rheanna Hall (7)
Hoyland Common Primary School

Ten Little Children

Ten little children
Looking mighty fine
Along came a giant
And then there were nine.

Nine little children
Going through a gate
Along came a hound dog
And then there were eight.

Eight little children
Counting to eleven
Along came a ghost
And then there were seven.

Seven little children
Picking up sticks
Along came a big kid
And then there were six.

Six little children
Looking in a hive
Along came a lot of bees
And then there were five.

Five little children
Whose feet are sore
Along came a blackbird
And then there were four.

Four little children
Who can't see
Along came a vampire
And then there were three.
Three little children
Who have the flu
Along came Daddy
And then there were two.

Two little children
Standing alone
Along came Mum
And then there was one.

Sophie Hodson (7)
Hoyland Common Primary School

ALPHABET POEM

A is for Ann who is very tidy
B is for Bob who acts very strange
C is for Chantelle who likes to write things down
D is for David who likes to jump in puddles
E is for Emma who runs after boys
F is for Fred who is very messy
G is for George who is very quiet
H is for Holly who likes reading books.

Robert Crowther (8)
Hoyland Common Primary School

HUNGER POEM

The veins pushing out of my skin
My heart going wild.
I can hardly breathe,
The blood going cold in my heart
All the pain inside me like I am dying
All the hate inside me is like a disease
My skin going red raw.

Adam Hinkles (9)
Hoyland Common Primary School

My Alphabet Poem

A is for Aiden who does lots of things.
B is for Barry who cleans all the bins.
C is for Carly who is rude.
D is for Derek who's not in the mood.
E is for everyone who loves each other.
F is for friends who have one mother.
G is for God who created all the world.
H is for hail which makes everyone curl.
I is for illness which doctors cure.
J is for joy which you don't have when you're in the sewer
K is for kissing which is used on Valentine's Day
L is for lying on the warm hay.

Aiden Birks (8)
Hoyland Common Primary School

Feeling Poem

Love is when you tease somebody.
Love is when you have a crush.
Love is when you have a Valentine's.
Love is when you fancy somebody.

Happiness is when you're having fun.
Happiness is a furry bunny.
Happiness is when you buy a toy.
Happiness is a really good friend.

Anger is when you have no friends.
Anger is when you're grounded.
Anger is when you're fed up.
Anger is when you're in trouble.

Ashley Sanderson (9)
Hoyland Common Primary School

AN ALPHABET POEM

A is for Amelia
Who has short hair.
B is for Brett
Who has a teddy bear.
C is for Chantelle
Who is really funny.
D is for Danny
Who is a big bully.
E is for Elliott
Who hates baths.
F is for Fred
Who always laughs.
G is for Georgina
Who was at my old school.
H is for Harriet
Who loves swimming pools.

Hollie Sylvester (8)
Hoyland Common Primary School

A NAME POEM

A is for Amelia
Who jumped in a puddle.

B is for Brett
Who got in a muddle.

C is for Chantelle
Who is very nice.

D is for Danny
Who is scared of mice.

E is for Elliott
Who is very silly.

F is for Fred
Who has a cousin called Billy.

G is for Georgia
Who loves toys.

H is for Hollie
Who doesn't like boys.

Robbin Evans (9)
Hoyland Common Primary School

A NAME POEM

A is for Amelia
Who finished a puzzle.
B is for Bridie
Who fell in a puddle.
C is for Chantelle
Who is very loud.
D is for Dad
Who sits around.
E is for Eden
Who always sings.
F is for Fred
Who thinks he's got wings.
G is for Georgia
Who is very nutty.
H is for Hollie
Who's always in a hurry.

Amelia Goodair (8)
Hoyland Common Primary School

ANIMAL ALPHABET POEM

A is for ant
B is for bear
C is for cat
D is for dog
E is for eggs
F is for funny animals
G is for goats
H is for horse
I is for insect
J is for jaguar
K is for kangaroo
L is for lizard
M is for monkey
N is for nuts animals eat
O is for owl
P is the piglet
Q is for queen bee
R is for rabbit
S is for snake
T is for tarantula
U is for ugly animals
V is for violent animals
W is for Wednesday when bats come out
X is for X-ray
Y is for yoghurt we get from animals
Z is for zebra.

Natalie Briscoe (8)
Hoyland Common Primary School

ALPHABET POEM (BOYS)

A is for Antony
he's my man.

B is for Ben
he gets the ham.

C is for Craig
who likes dancing.

D is for Danny
who's always prancing.

E is for Eddi
who's cute as can be.

F is for Father
who's forever for me.

G is for Greg
who loves chips.

H is for Harry
who always spits.

I is for Ian
he loves pies.

J is for Jimmy
who's crazy about rides.

K is for Ken
who's got a friend, Twix.

L is Len
who loves tricks.

M is for Morris
who loves pets.

N is for Norris
who always bets.
O is for Orbit

who wants me.

P is for Peter
who keeps a flea.

Q is for Qwen
who says when.

R is for Rex
who loves his own den.

S is for Stuart
who's got a dog Jack.

T is for Ted
who's got a lumpy back.

U is for Urn
who's got a stroppy cat.

V is for Venson
who's got a six pack.

W is for Wayne
who really love me.

X is for X-ray
who hates tea.

Y is for Yo-yo
who kisses you.

Z is for Zack
who loves me too.

Sarah Newbold (9)
Hoyland Common Primary School

MY FRIENDS' NAMES

A is for Abi
Who hates boys.

B is for Bethan
Who likes to play with toys.

C is for Chantelle
Who has very short hair.

D is for Danny
Who likes bears.

E is for Emma
Who likes to pray.

F is for Fred
Who has got a dad
Called Ray.

G is for Georgia
Who plays with me.

H is for Hayley
Who hurt her knee.

Chloe Levers (8)
Hoyland Common Primary School

THE MOON

The moon is a calm person,
She glows over homeless children like an angel shining,
She is a god that protects everything in darkness,
She smiles as the god of heat disappears,
Her beaming eyes shine light on the lost sailors,
She fights with darkness,
Trying to make the night light as the sun moves up,
And she disappears till the next night.

Kyle Reese Thomas (11)
Hoyland Common Primary School

VOLCANO

The evil beast crawls with anger,
The giant starts to roar.
The evil man spews with anger,
Burning all around.
The evil devil roars with laughter,
Enjoying it more and more.

The evil devil's matted beard,
Drooped right over the land.
His poisonous breath rose higher and higher,
Poisoning all the trees.

As it rains more and more,
All the rage will fade.
The evil devil goes down to death,
Turns to smoke and is never seen again.

Ian Uttley (10)
Hoyland Common Primary School

THE VOLCANO

The volcano's lava slid down the volcano's side,
Nothing can stop its path.
The dust grabs and suffocates with its pointy hands,
Then the lava burns you to death.

The volcano's smoking head,
Firing fiery rocks.
The volcano's red, angry eyes,
Glooming, bloodshot eyes.

A booming deep echoing voice
Burning the city like a boot crushing cans.
The beast is asleep.

Ben McNamara (10)
Hoyland Common Primary School

THE SEA

The sea was very angry.
His waves came tumbling over.
He tortured the beach
And everyone ran
And none of them came again.
Then one little girl ran down
The steps.
The sea was
Very angry still and his
Tight claws clutched
And took the girl away
And she was
Never seen
Again.

Stacey Jayne Rooney (10)
Hoyland Common Primary School

BONFIRE

Snapping old logs and trees,
Roaring like a bloodthirsty lion
Into the distance,
The angry beast devoured the dead leaves.
The beast viciously
Ripped the wood to shreds,
If I watch I can see him
Winking an angry red eye,
He is roaring his head off.

Ben Dyer (9)
Hoyland Common Primary School

THE SEA

The sea's echo travels along the beach.
Its glowing eyes appear
In the rushing waves.
The thunder makes him get angry,
As more water rushes onto him.

The gloomy, sad-hearted young man screams
With anger and he gets bigger and runs faster.
Then the sun comes out
And the sea calms down again.

Chantelle Selby (10)
Hoyland Common Primary School

THE VOLCANO

He creeps up slowly to the hole in his face,
He spews out fiery red lava.
He devours things that get in his way.
His smoky beard takes over the air,
Suffocating the people below.

Now he spreads the red-hot lava,
Turning things to stones.
His bloodshot eyes just stare and stare.
He doesn't care what he has done.

Now the ash is being blown away,
But the ash doesn't want to go.
His voice echoing, 'I'll be back,
To devour those who stand in my way.'

Rebecca Drew (11)
Hoyland Common Primary School

THE VOLCANO

He is calm and quiet.
He sleeps like a baby as
He rests in peace.

Then he spews out deadly gases.
Boiling lava gushes down the
Mountainous volcano.

He devours everything in his path.
An evil face appears.
Scorching red eyes stare at me.

Everything becomes calm.
He once more settles down to
Rest in peace.

Laura Chipchase (11)
Hoyland Common Primary School

THE SEA

The sea was as steady as a rock
Until . . .
Boom, bang against the cliff
Like clenching fists.
The deep hollow voice was shouting
And screaming like a baby crying for milk.
Then he stopped. It went very peaceful
Like someone fast asleep
He dropped and dropped
Splash!
Then everyone went to the beach and had
A nice day.

Lauren Oxborrow (10)
Hoyland Common Primary School

THE VOLCANO

The volcano is a grumpy old man who spews out lava and dust,
Then a deadly face rises up with the poisonous gas that comes
out of his head.
His face looks over the people with the bloodshot, gloomy eyes.
His voice is deep and hollow, the sound of an echoing voice.
His hair is straggly, it's burning. He stays there, in the same place.
He looks over everything, thinking when to spill the lava
and devour everything in sight.

Courtney Hayles (10)
Hoyland Common Primary School

JESSICA

J   is for just so pretty.
E   is for excellent.
S   is for sweet.
S   is for success.
I   is for intelligent.
C   is for celebrating Jessica's new age.
A   is for achievements.

I really like Jessica a lot,
She's really good when it comes to a knot.
She's always there for me,
Her favourite drink is a cup of tea.

Chantelle Palmer (10)
Kexborough Primary School

MY BEST FRIEND JAMES

J   is for joy.
A   is for always.
M   is for mischievous.
E   is for excellent listener.
S   is for support.

Kimberly Robertshaw (10)
Kexborough Primary School

MY GRANDAD IKE

(In loving memory of a loving grandfather
who passed away shortly after this poem
was written)

My grandad is rose red,
He is a comfy cushion.
My grandad is as big as a hippopotamus,
He is a light in the dark.
My grandad is a path to the land of vegetables,
He is my grandad Ike.

Luke Taylor (10)
Kexborough Primary School

THE OCEAN MEADOW

Clouds hiding to make the day perfect,
Sky floating above like an ocean of blue.
Swathes of grass waving in the breeze
Like dancing seaweed weighed down with dew.

A fallen log in and among the grass,
But it became, for one brief moment, a shipwreck!
Laying half buried down on the seabed
Fungus-like coral flourishing upon the rotting deck.

Leaves rustling on nearby trees like the roar of the sea,
White and pink clover littering the earth like scallop shells.
Scurrying beetles became crabs in their armour,
The colour of the ocean, the blue of harebells.

A recent shower left a rainbow, a reef of colour,
Shoals of flashing fish like a multicoloured arc.
A disturbed bee landed upon a flower,
Buzzzzzz, a wide open mouth - *shark!*

Sarah Hill (11)
Kexborough Primary School

THE AIR AND WIND

The wind whistled a strong tune in the air,
It travelled country to country
And town to town.
It travelled faster than lightning
But slower than a plane.

When the wind blows
The trees are happy,
They know it is time
For swaying and dancing.

Timothy Newman (9)
Kexborough Primary School

A FRIEND

A friend is what you are
And what you shall always be.
They're always there for you
When you're feeling down.

A friend is so adoring
But some are just so boring,
Some are very happy too,
I'll always be your friend.

Stacey Peace (10)
Kexborough Primary School

MY FRIEND KIMBERLY

K   is for kind.
I   is for intelligent.
M   is for my friend.
B   is for brainy.
E   is for exciting.
R   is for radiant.
L   is for lovely.
Y   is for you, Kimberly.

Emma Harding (10)
Kexborough Primary School

IN THE DARK

In the dark it's very gloomy.
In the dark there is no light.
In the dark I need my teddy
Because it's in the night.

In the dark I'm very lonely
But my teddy gives me a hug.
In the dark I'm very sleepy,
Then when I'm asleep I'm like a bug.

When I'm asleep my alarm sets off,
I rub my eyes and doze back off.
Mum shouts, 'Up time.' I shout, 'No!'
Then I pretend I have a cough.

Lauren Cowley (9)
Kexborough Primary School

WHEN THE RAIN FALLS

W ater is blue,
H ouses shelter us,
E agles fly with the rain,
N ice is the rain as it falls to the ground.

T he rain feels cold as the wind blows it down,
H ouses stop us from getting wet,
E arth has water,

R aindrops falling,
A s the rain falls
I t feels cold,
N icely the rain settles on the ground.

F resh it all feels when the rain has gone,
A s it falls you can feel it on your hands,
L eaves blow,
L ovely and wet,
S un and rain make a rainbow.

Melissa Russell (8)
Kexborough Primary School

When The Rain Falls

When the rain falls I can hear
Splash, splash, pitter, pat, drip, drop.
I can hear God in my mind,
Too many people have done wrong
And this is the punishment.

When the rain falls I can see
Little tiny droplets falling from the sky.
In my mind I can see God wearing a frown
And people throwing a tantrum.

When the rain falls I can smell
Smoke like a fire burning,
Rotten cheese smelling in the fridge, orange juice bubbling.
God can let down a fresh smell after the rain has gone.

When the rain falls I feel sad and mad,
Angry, frustrated, furious, grotty and bad.
God says, 'Don't get mad, people are sad,
It won't go on.'

Sophie Walker (9)
Kexborough Primary School

Holding The Baby

I was at Rochdale,
It was at Richmale House,
A baby cries, a baby screams,
A baby plays, a baby paddies.
A baby has names, a baby has pains,
A baby has a dummy, a baby has a mummy,
I was scared, I was flared,
The baby wears posh clothes.

Emily Anne Cowley (8)
Kexborough Primary School

Rain Works Wonders

R ain is vital.
A pples and pears grow from the seeds for it.
I t gives us life.
N othing can live without it.

W hen it rains we enjoy it.
O ceans and seas are filled with rain.
R ivers give space for it.
K ind God made rain.
S now falls in cold weather.

W ater is a miraculous creation.
O f course rain is a liquid.
N obody should waste it.
D ripping on roofs.
E very drop counts.
R ain is wonderful.
S unlight evaporates it.

Daniel Booth (9)
Kexborough Primary School

My Gran Poem

My gran is as small as a puppy.
Her hair is like wool.
Her eyes are like marbles.
Her face is like a wrinkly old dog.
When she walks she is as slow as a slug.
When she sits she is like a bent stick.
When she laughs she is like a hyena.
When she sleeps she is like a snoring pig.
The best thing about my gran is that she loves me a lot.

Abby Potter (8)
Kexborough Primary School

HOLDING A BABY

My parents said I could have a baby photo
Taken with my newborn sister,
When I held her she felt light,
But sometimes she's annoying,
She screams and cries every night.
When I looked she was kinda cute,
Just wriggling and squiggling like a newt,
Click! Click!
I just want to see what the photo looks like,
I feel happy,
But a bit jealous though,
Because Mum and Dad had said be careful,
She's only a little tyke.

Jennifer Rhodes (8)
Kexborough Primary School

FISHERMEN

Fishermen fish.
Sea bash, sea crash.
Boats float, boats fish.
Sea sparkle, sea calm.
Shells glitter, shells sink.
Sea blue, sea salty.
Starfish curl, starfish still.
Sea waves, sea bright.
Sunrise, sunset.
Fishermen fish.

Kris Cookson (9)
Kexborough Primary School

WAVES CRASH, WAVES SMASH

Waves crash, waves smash
on the seashore.
Waves crash, waves smash
on the promenade floor.
Waves crash, waves smash
all day long.
Waves crash, waves smash
until the day's gone.

Waves crash, waves smash
night and day.
Waves crash, waves smash,
they won't go away.
Waves crash, waves smash
fierce and loud.
Waves crash, waves smash
wetting a loud crowd.

Jordan Sykes (8)
Kexborough Primary School

IN MEMORY OF MY AUNTIE SUSAN

Trudy and Sam were Susan's best friends,
She cradled them most nights at the foot of her bed.
Sam was her doll that she loved very much,
Trudy was her teddy that she got while she was ill
And was at her bedside while she was dying!
It was very hard for me that day,
The day my auntie passed away.

For Susan was one of my best friends,
She was my best auntie too,
For we loved to dance to Susan's best songs.
Susan loved my brothers too
And now she will miss Jordan learn to walk
And all of us growing up too.

Susan was like a child at heart
With a lot of things to do,
She let me play with her and her toys,
We played like friends do.

I know she's gone to a better place
With a lot of angels to watch over her,
I'm going to miss my Auntie Susan very, very much.

Hayley Coldwell (9)
Kexborough Primary School

WAR

What is this life if full of war?
Why is there not any peace anymore?
People die and lose their lives.
I wish there was not war
So people keep safe and don't die.
It causes unhappiness and splits up families,
It causes trouble and it's very noisy,
Wars are nasty.

James Saxton (8)
Kexborough Primary School

SEA POEM

Waves crash, fish splash.
Waves bump, fish jump.
Seagulls fly, fishermen are shy.
Water flows, wind blows.
Fishermen catch, crabs snatch.
Storms come, fishermen are done.

Sam Harding (9)
Kexborough Primary School

MY BROTHER

My little brother is as cute as can be,
At times he really infuriates me!
From angel to devil
In the blink of an eye.
'Who tore my picture?'
'Not me,' he will cry.
Tiny fingers, tiny toes,
Rosebud mouth, button nose.
Fast asleep or wide awake
He steals my heart,
But for goodness sake
Give me a break.

James Hinchcliffe (10)
Kexborough Primary School

FEELINGS

When feelings are great they're nicer than anything
That you could wish for in your heart.
Feelings can be down or they can be up.
Feelings are in my heart all the time.

Feelings are for happiness and joy,
You can only use feelings in a certain time or place.
Feelings are brilliant to use at any time at all or in any place.

Sometimes we can use them when we are sad
Or when we're feeling down.
We should use feelings properly.

Edward Plant (9)
Kexborough Primary School

WHO BROKE IT?

I used to play an instrument
When I was just aged 10.
I'd take it home to practise,
Then fetch it back again.

I took it home one evening
And practised just a bit,
Then left it out of its case
And shouted, 'Who broke it?'

I took it back to school next day
Shaking like a newborn cat,
I'd took it back all broken
And I thought that was that!

I continued with my lessons
And got my violin mended,
He fixed it that same day
And I thought it was splendid.

April Lodge (10)
Kexborough Primary School

THE SUN AND RAIN

T he shiny sun shines,
H oping the sun will never go down,
E nding the sun and out comes the rain.

S lowly a rainbow appears in the sky,
U nderneath the clouds appears a . . .
N ice lot of colours, the colours of red, silver, gold,

S apphire, yellow, pink, green, purple, orange and
H oping that the colour blue appears . . .
I n the rainbow,
N ow the rainbow disappears, it
E nds the day,
S o please thank God for the sun and rain.

Michaela Russell (9)
Kexborough Primary School

SPRING

Sound the flute!
Now it's mute.
Bird delight,
Day and night,
Nightingale
In the dale,
Lark in sky,
Merrily,
Merrily, merrily to welcome in the year.

Little boy
Full of joy,
Little girl
Sweet and small,
Cock does crow,
So do you.
Merry voice,
Infant noise,
Merrily, merrily to welcome in the year.

Jody Moore (11)
Kexborough Primary School

THIS MORNING

I heard my mum get up,
She went down the stairs,
I heard her make a cup of tea,
I heard her drag a chair.

I heard my sister get up,
She was turning the TV on,
I heard her put her clothes on,
I turned around and she was gone.

I heard the wind howling,
I heard a bird singing,
I heard the leaves crunching,
I heard a bell dinging.

I heard my dog barking,
My dog was crying,
I heard my mum shouting
And I was sighing.

I heard my sister put her shoe on,
I heard her shout, 'Bye, bye.'
Then she shouted me
And then I shouted, 'Why?'

Kealy Hutchinson (8)
Kexborough Primary School

SLOWLY

I slowly drift up away and away,
We are slower than the birds in the sky today.
I then look above
And see a white dove,
Fluttering, fluttering away he does,
Trying to get away from all of us.
River deep,
Mountain high,
Down below not in the sky.
We flutter down
Making no sound.
We've had a great day
And we will see you again in May!

Eleanor Smith (10)
Kexborough Primary School

A CHRISTMAS PROMISE

Christmas carollers run riot on the 20th
Gathering money for gifts and presents.
Sweet young voices travel through the frosty night
Giving people a memory to cherish.

Parents marching in the town centre,
Rushing and buying out all the shops.
Everybody fighting over one thing or another
In the hustle and bustle of Christmastime.

Christmas Day has finally come,
The house of kindness is full of litter.
Santa Claus came late last night
And kept his Christmas promise.

Ben Bentley (11)
Kexborough Primary School

A SWALEDALE VILLAGE

Listen!
What can you hear?
The hoot of an owl in the still of the night,
The gentle rustle of leaves in the breeze.

Listen!
What can you hear?
The song of the river tumbling down the steep fall,
The sound of cattle mooing on their way to the dairy.

Listen!
What can you hear?
The distant bleat of sheep on the high hill tops,
The rumble of a tractor climbing up the steep slope to collect them.

Listen!
What can you hear?
The sweet sound of birds tweeting high up in the sky,
The muffled crunch of walkers' boots on the shifting stones.

Nicola Dinsdale (8)
Kexborough Primary School

NUMBER TIME

'Twas midnight in the classroom
And everywhere was dark
When suddenly from a number square
Was a heard a smart remark.

Said one to two, 'I don't like you
You really are a horror,
Whenever you need something
You never seem to borrow.'

Said three to four, 'I agree,
I do think she's a pain,
I'd rather be somewhere else
Or underneath a train.'

Rebecca Senior (10)
Kexborough Primary School

A Trip To The Zoo

At the zoo there's loads
Of animals,
But they're in cages.

At the zoo there are
Cheeky monkeys, parakeets,
Zebras, polar bears
And giraffes.

I like nearly all the animals
But there are lions and tigers
That I don't like.

The growl and roar.
The lions are orange
And the giraffes are a yellow colour.

A zebra is white and black,
Polar bears are white
And monkey are brown.

Rebecca Jessop (9)
Kexborough Primary School

In The Dark, Dark Garden

In the dark, dark garden you see trees and flowers.
In the dark, dark garden not one creature creaks.
In the dark, dark garden every creature creaks.
In the dark, dark garden every creature sleeps.
In the dark, dark garden there are birds, one is in a tree.
In the dark, dark garden every creature goes to sleep.

Brendan Chopra (10)
Kexborough Primary School

SUMMER

S   ummer's sun sets,
U   ndoutable sun,
M   ornings are bright,
M   erry time of year,
E   ven better than spring,
R   inging bells everywhere.

Matthew Niland (9)
Kexborough Primary School

DARKNESS

I scare the wits out of siblings
As lightness fades away,
Humid winds fill the welking
As children lay awake,
Dark, ghostly, fearless, dull.

I walk the streets
Turning things to pitch-black,
I make you petrified,
I make you shiver,
Dark, ghostly, fearless, dull.

I hear the birds twittering
So I force myself down,
It's time for sunrise,
I move round the world,
Dark, ghostly, fearless, dull.

Amy Barlow (11)
Owston Skellow Junior School

WORLD WAR I

20th century declares World War I,
Men gather round for our nation,
Training to be strapping soldiers
Working for the land.

Waiting for their silent death
In deep, murky trenches.
Soldiers are painfully dying
With their lives still to start.

Forces of the general
Make the nervous wrecks sweat.
'Out you go! Over the top!'
They take their last breath.

Bullets left, right and centre,
Coming closer to live flesh.
Now the time has come
For their silent death.

Death's door has opened,
Their soul has passed them by.

Katie Astbury (11)
Owston Skellow Junior School

FEAR

Fear is like your inner soul, your weaknesses
That come alive and shock you, scare you and even kill you.
Here's some of the worst fears in phrases.
The tall, dark figure glared as he stood holding a sword
In his hand with blood dripping off drop by drop, drop by drop,
A man with a white mask on and a chainsaw at the end of your landing.

Fear picks at your weaknesses until you're terrorised,
You're that scared you daren't open your bedroom door,
Just to go the bathroom for a drink so you hold it in
For as long as you can, but some people can't handle it.
They stay still in their bed and shiver, they don't blink,
They just hope that light will come soon.

Fears don't just happen at night, some happen in the day,
Some aren't our imagination, some are real life problems,
For example small spaces, claustrophobia.
Another example is spiders, it is called arachnophobia,
Some can be cats, some can be dogs,
Mice, rats and even tortoises.

Fears are all over the world, everyone has them,
Some already know, but some still haven't found it out,
Sometimes people have height problems.
People have air problems but we hope,
People can face up to their fear and destroy it.

Blake Siddall (11)
Owston Skellow Junior School

FEARS

As I stand on the jagged edge of the gargantuan cliff
My fear makes me tremble.
I dread when I see things
Because my fear mounts up and I scream.

When I see a skeleton walk by my bedroom
It is like a blazing flame going up my spine.
I dread going up the back alley
Night after night.

Every night I check that the doors are locked
Before I go straight to bed,
Just in case someone nearby approaches the house,
It terrifies me if I leave the doors unlocked.

My fear is like a ghost going straight through my body,
Some people suffer with fears
Such as being alone in the dark
And other things.

Everyone in the world has fears,
Some people have bad fears,
Some people are not that afraid,
So I hope all people get through their fears.

Greg Andrew Smith (10)
Owston Skellow Junior School

THUNDER AND LIGHTNING

The clouded sky was filled with rage
Like a lion trapped inside a cage.
It burst free with a deafening roar,
A roaring flash comes before.

The screeching blare was mighty boomy,
The illuminated sky was rather gloomy,
Dashes flew at the speed of light,
The lion pounced with all its might.

The rumble grew as the night ticked passed,
The torching light became extremely vast,
Then the lion bellowed with pain,
After there were trickles of rain.

Soon the lightning was of mass destruction
Like a tornado losing all power and suction.
After the lion belted out a cry,
It was losing all power but refused to die.

Brooke Vickers (10)
Owston Skellow Junior School

THE DESERT

The desert is like a cage of fury,
Demons of Satan guard its lands,
The claws of death snatch the intruder
And keep him locked in the scorching sands.

The winds work with the malevolent demons,
It races across the dusty plains,
The speed grew as it hurtled through the desert,
Chewing and spitting out sand grains.

It starves for a wandering soul
To keep imprisoned in the cage,
It feeds on pain and suffering
To build up its mighty rage.

Laura Kirby (11)
Owston Skellow Junior School

A TYPICAL DAY AT SCHOOL

School starts at half-past eight,
Lots of people are always late.
Ring, ring, there goes the bell,
Better not move or someone will tell.

Sitting in the classroom,
Waiting for the call,
Line up quietly
And go into the hall.

Going to assembly
In single file,
We all know we'll be sat there
For a little while.

Back in the classroom
Getting ready for maths,
Everyone gets their rulers out
Because it's time for graphs.

Ring, ring, there it goes again,
But it's a wet break,
They are always a pain.

Next lesson's a reading comp,
They are really long,
But they always get worse
When the teacher sings a song.
Next thing's dinner time,
We all sit down for lunch,
Oh no, not again,
The pudding's chocolate crunch.

At quarter to one lessons start,
Science, RE and then some art.
Waiting for the home time bell,
Now it's time to raise some hell.

Josh Clark (11)
Owston Skellow Junior School

RAPIDLY THE TORNADO . . .

Rapidly the tornado
Is ripping up the fields,
Smashing his arm across the grass,
Spinning, spinning
His mighty body destroying all around,
Thumping his feet around the village,
Whirling, whirling,
A sprinter running for a medal.

Jakir Hussain (11)
Phillimore Park Primary School

SOFTLY THE SNOW

Tight curly beard with a red nose,
Fingertips spreading, searching the land.
Past the sleepy bedrooms and the shimmering sky,
Tiptoeing down the dusty chimneys,
Sneaking away from the reindeers.
Twinkling, twinkling,
Tight curly beard and a red nose.
Sparkling, sparkling
On the rooftops.
Slowly the snow,
Snow drops left by the fire,
Place the snow likes to be.
Softly the snow,
Father Christmas hunting in his red clothes.

Michelle Morrissey (11)
Phillimore Park Primary School

TWINKLY THE ICE-WHITE SNOW

Twinkly ice-white snow,
Frozen white teeth and white grey hair,
Arms touching the frozen hard grass,
Past the crying snow of the gentle old bench,
Through the wrecked old houses,
On the white frozen cheeks,
Eyes twitching over broken old, rusty, frozen glasses,
Twinkly ice-white snow,
Touching, touching,
Spreading its white sparkly breath
On a wrinkly old mouth,
Crying, crying,
Twinkly ice-white snow,
A child crying over a broken toy.

Savannah Mayo (10)
Phillimore Park Primary School

QUICKLY THE THUNDER

Quickly the thunder,
Huge gigantic feet,
Claws gigantic,
Don't know where to go,
Belly rumbling,
Don't know where to find food,
Where is it?
He does not know.
Quick the thunder,
Destroy! Destroy
In the winter across the dark house
Bullying, bullying,
Leaving a hungry man and woman
Trying to find a meal.

Lorna Meeds (11)
Phillimore Park Primary School

CRAZILY THE THUNDER

Crazily the thunder,
Rumbling belly with a screaming mouth,
Crashing and tearing through towns and woods,
Across the houses and gardens in a zooming flash.
Crazily the thunder,
Charging, charging
Here and there,
Threatening, threatening,
The howling wind,
Crazily the thunder,
A mad man exploring the world.

Fateha Zaman (11)
Phillimore Park Primary School

MADLY THE THUNDER

Madly the thunder
Howling through my door,
Stopping my unconscious sleep.
Madly the thunder
Flashing, crashing
Around the countryside
Sounds like a deep rumbling volcano.
Madly the thunder
Smashing, smashing
All the garden gates,
Crossing the woods, interrupting the animals sleep,
His hungry belly rumbling for food,
A starving man searching for his dinner.

Nipa Begum (11)
Phillimore Park Primary School

QUICKLY THE THUNDER

Quickly the thunder
Kicking feet over houses,
Arms crashing about,
Through the towns, past houses,
Destroying trees, power-cut,
Wrecking gardens with pink roses.
Quickly the thunder
Shaking, shaking,
Invisibly moving through skies
Grabbing, grabbing,
Hands grabbing my dad's tie.
Quickly the thunder,
A mad man robbing the bank.

Natasha Mirza (11)
Phillimore Park Primary School

CAN YOU GUESS?

It's colourful and bright,
It blows in the wind,
All sizes and shapes.

It goes up and down,
Round and round,
Blowing high and low.

Flying like a jet plane
Colour mix,
Green, blue, red and yellow.

Ribbons and curls,
Spirals and plaits,
Bows and shapes hanging.

You've guessed it's a kite!

Sarah Wells (9)
St Mary's RC Primary School, Sheffield

I NEVER RAISED MY BOY TO BE A SOLDIER

(Based on the song 'I Didn't Raise My Son To Be A Soldier')

I never raised my boy to be a solider,
I know I'm going to be very proud of him,
I hope he comes back
With his gun and his sack
'Cause I never raised my boy to be a soldier.

I never raised my boy to be a soldier,
I never forgot his toy McKoy,
I know he'll always be my baby,
My little baby boy.

I never raised my boy to be a soldier,
I hope he comes back nice and safe,
He'll always be a pleasure
With his love and his leisure
'Cause I never raised my boy to be a soldier.

Paul Burgin (10)
St Mary's RC Primary School, Sheffield

I NEVER . . .

(Based on the Song 'I Didn't Raise My Son To Be A Soldier')

I never raised my boy to be a soldier,
I never thought I'd have an empty heart.
It feels so bad, it's so not fair,
I never thought my boy and me would part.

I never raised my boy to be a soldier,
I feel so incredibly mixed up.
My poor, poor boy, I feel so bad
And this is just my luck.

I never raised my boy to be a soldier,
I never thought I'd feel this loneliness,
I never thought I'd feel this upset,
Why have I got this unhappiness?

I never raised my boy to be a soldier,
When will he be able to come back?
Can I have more time with him?
Army general please give him the sack.

Hannah McShane (10)
St Mary's RC Primary School, Sheffield

THE LADY OF SHALOTT
(Based on 'The Lady Of Shalott' by Alfred Lord Tennyson)

'The curse is upon me,' cried the Lady of Shalott.
There were some shivers and shakes
As more of the glass mirror breaks,
Now more noises she makes,
The Lady of Shalott.
Now the turrets are falling out,
As Lancelot heard a great shout
More rumbling came from the great mount
Of the island Shalott.

The towers are crashing to the ground,
As more of the terrible sound,
Howling noises like a hound
Come from the mirror broken
And on the wooden wall behind
The Lady of Shalott will find,
Something to rattle up her mind
On the broken mirror's wall.

Lancelot hears the terror
As he comes to save her,
He earns no wager,
Saving the day.
He runs out of the castle door,
Across the drawbridge on the moor,
He stares with a heart broken -
And he saw
The Lady of Shalott is no more.

Ben Thompson (10)
St Mary's RC Primary School, Sheffield

THE Y5 RAP

We're the coolest class this school's ever seen,
We're the hip hop, tip top rapping machine.

We're the coolest class in all of the school,
Everyone says that we are cool,
We rap outside even if it rains,
Our parents think that we are pains.

We rap all night, we rap all day,
We're the best class, you should say.
We act like fools at the swimming pools,
So just say that Y5 rules.

Callum Warburton (9)
St Mary's RC Primary School, Sheffield

THE BLITZ

Hear the sound of the gun.
Hear the cry of the young.
See the bombs exploding.
See the houses falling.

See the people crawling.
See the people falling.
See the people crying.
See the people dying.
See the aeroplanes flying.

Hear the sound of men fighting.
Hear the sound of men shouting.
Hear the sound of babies' crying
And hear the siren ringing.

Callum Holden (10)
St Mary's RC Primary School, Sheffield

THE LADY OF SHALOTT

(Based on 'The Lady Of Shalott' by Alfred Lord Tennyson)

'The curse is upon me,' cried the Lady of Shalott.

She got punished and got the blame
And people thought all the same.
Lancelot looked up her shame,
The lady knew that all her fame
Was banished from Camelot.
So Lancelot took her away,
'O how on earth shall I repay?'
The lady cried and tried to say,
What O' what did I decay?
To Lancelot she cried and knelt,
Her heart soon began to melt,
She did not know for what to ask
And knew this was no easy task,
Not for the Lady of Shalott.
Locked in the dungeons she cried and cried,
Alive she did so hard she tried,
But could not last and so she died,
Yes, the Lady of Shalott,
But still in the castle her soul was there
And so she haunts the prison heir.
At night her voice moans and cries
And on her bed her body lies -
Of course, The Lady of Shalott!

Jasmine Lobo (10)
St Mary's RC Primary School, Sheffield

MY HAIKU

The sun is beaming
Water's is evaporating
Up into the clouds.

Water is falling
On a mountain in the ground
Goes in-between rocks.

Meandering down
Going down under bridges
Going in a lake.

Going in a mill
Getting a great waterfall
Water gone downfall.

Ryan Jacobs (10)
St Mary's RC Primary School, Sheffield

WAVES

Waves jumping up high,
Claws like scaled monster,
Swinging on the sand.

Reducing calm sea,
Swirling in and out of rocks,
Peaceful, gentle sea.

Danger for your life,
The slushy sand is lively,
Waterfalls are rough.

Trickling seashore,
Flowing calmly with the fishes,
Singing up and down.

'*Slam, crash,*' says the sea,
Rocks are breaking here and there,
Now the sea is calm.

Felicity Deighton (10)
St Mary's RC Primary School, Sheffield

THE SONG OF HIAWATHA

A new baby is born
at the crack of dawn
'What shall we call him,
my darling Kym?'
'Hiawatha!'

Got to go to sleep
and don't make a peep,
Be a good son if you
want to have fun
'Hiawatha.'

It is too hot. Fire!
get Hiawatha out of his cot.
My husband is dead
he lay his sweet head
'Hiawatha.'

Three years after,
there was no more laughter.
His parents had died
So he cried,
'Hiawatha!'

Antonia Mitchell (10)
St Mary's RC Primary School, Sheffield

Y5 RAP

Chorus
We're the coolest class the school's ever seen,
We're the hip hop, tip top rapping machine.

The school is so boring, that's why we are here,
So you'd better be ready cos you're about to disappear.
Make it good, we don't have any time
Especially for you, when you seem to whine.

Chorus

Miss Cole likes guinea pigs
She's got one called Bart,
But I think he's got a really cold heart.
Now where should I start?
I think he boogies alone in the dark.

Chorus

Mr Hopkins likes singing every day, sometimes
we find him a real big pain.
He embarrasses us at dinner time and
that's the part when we start to whine.

Chorus.

Zoë Muscat (9)
St Mary's RC Primary School, Sheffield

EVACUATION CHILD

E veryone wondering why they're leaving Mum and Dad,
V ery dull, dark and grey faces. Very sad.
A ll the children have a tag,
C hildren hold a small bag.
U nited one day, will the mothers be,
A ll children I'm sure, will one day see
T he trains are noisy, loud and hooting
I nside children are safe, outside guns are shooting.
O n arrival, smiling faces
N ow children think of scary places.

C aring not much, leave the boy
H eartbroken left with Mrs McKoy.
I nside he felt scared
L onely, sad, like nobody cared.
D reaming, he saw his mum weeping thinking
he could come back home. When he woke up
and saw the reality of war.

Alice Morrisey (10)
St Mary's RC Primary School, Sheffield

WAR IS DECLARED

Lots and lots of people crying
Even more people dying
Lots and lots of people who are sad
Adolph Hitler is very glad.

People listening to the radio
Hearing that war is declared
Even though it's going to snow
Families are getting prepared.

War is now definitely declared
People getting very scared
Adults watching their kids go
As well as shouting, 'No, no, no!'

War is won -
There's the sun.
We've won, we've won,
We've won!

Siñead O'Grady (10)
St Mary's RC Primary School, Sheffield

THE THREE LITTLE PIGS

Mum told us it was time to go.
My big bro.
Wanted to go to Mexico.
Mum said, 'No!'
It was too far
because we weren't
allowed Dad's car.

The three little pigs gathered their stuff
and out they went, in a bit of a huff.

The first little piggy
made a house out of straw
because that was the first thing he saw.

The second little piggy picked up some sticks
whilst he was eating a chocolate Twix.

The third little piggy made a house out of bricks
because this little piggy was full of tricks.

Frances Morgan (10)
St Mary's RC Primary School, Sheffield

WATER NATURE

Trickling water
water, very refreshing.
Its nature is kind.

Water, very calm
its everlasting peace.
It runs through forests.

Falling waterfalls
running through mountains.
It goes like a butterfly.

Trickling in caves
streams coming through the forest,
Meandering round.

Running in-between
running down the mountain tops.
Falling over rocks.

Robert Unwin (10)
St Mary's RC Primary School, Sheffield

THE BLITZ

Planes bombing
This means war!
Houses crashing and burning
Children dying
Parents crying
Men fighting
Germans searching
Germans spying, poisonously
Guns firing

Hitler getting ready
Britons firing at Germans
Germans dying
Hitler dying
Britain winning and
Germany losing!

Chipo Marange (9)
St Mary's RC Primary School, Sheffield

THE CLASS FIVE RAP

Chorus
We're a wicked class, hardly anybody's seen,
We're a nip-nap touch yer cap, rapping machine

It's cooler than a fan
We're all friends, wicked man.
We'll rap all night
And we'll rap out of sight.

Chorus

We'll rap down the playground and through the field,
We'll go through the town like a metal shield.
We go to the town swimming pool
If you have a fight with us, you'll look like a fool.

Chorus

Joe Brown (9)
St Mary's RC Primary School, Sheffield

FORGET-ME-NOT

He's so cute and sensitive
I love him lots and lots.
He's the best flower in the world
My flower, the forget-me-not.

I'll never ever forget him
I'll stick to his name
But once I left him behind
In the pouring down rain.

Safely in my pocket
When I go to town
One day he even made me
Stop and listen to a clown!

By now he's very tired
So I send him up to bed
In a pot with lots of mud
And compost for his head.

Jessica Slingsby (10)
St Theresa's RC Primary School

INSIDE MY HEAD

When I get tucked in at night
I get a nasty thought in my head and I feel all funny.
I get frightened of the monster coming
And gobbling me up
And then I'd have to live in his tummy.

Pulling my pyjamas on
Sitting on the bed,
I slowly feel my legs
Getting pulled under the duvet.
The monster's tugging at my ankle
To live inside his tummy.

The night-time drags on
The hours tick slowly by
The gurglings and droolings of the monster,
Groan on and on.
My mind races, imagining the worst -
About living in his tummy.

The daylight begins to stream
Through the open curtains.
Monster shrieks and turns tail
Away from my nightmare.
I run downstairs for breakfast . . .
To fill up my empty tummy!

Dreamt by

Sarah Ward (11)
St Theresa's RC Primary School

MY FAVOURITE THINGS

I have a lot of favourite things,
They always come and go.
Sometimes they could be all around
Sometimes I just don't know!

Some days I like dogs with weird faces,
Maybe a frog that catches flies.
I have a lot of favourite things,
Whatever catches my eye.

A rainbow shining brightly,
The moon, lighting up the sky.
I have a lot of favourite things,
Whatever catches my eye!

Monique Norcliffe (11)
St Theresa's RC Primary School

FAVOURITE THINGS

Reading at night
Under the sheets,
One of my favourite things.

Swimming outside
In the pool,
One of my favourite things.

Having sleepovers
Whenever I like
One of my favourite things

But best of all, my favourite thing is
Spending time
With my mum and dad.

Jenny Griffin (10)
St Theresa's RC Primary School

MY ESSENTIAL PACK-IN SUITCASE

A   is for art equipment to paint a picture,
B   is for a bouncy ball to kick around the yard,
C   is for computers to play my games on.
D   is for doggies who go out on the streets,
E   is for empty stomachs, which are hungry.
F   is for frightened people, who are scared,
G   is for giants who are really big and scary.
H   is for the man in Steps the pop band who split up,
I   is for international, track and field events,
J   is for Jordan - my name.
K   is for King Henry VIII,
L   is for lion, roaring loudly.
M   is for the Milky Way out in space.
N   is for the nosy boy,
O   is for octopus with eight hairy legs,
P   is for peas which we eat.
Q   is for the Queen Mother who is in Heaven.
R   is for Ronaldo, who plays for Brazil.
S   is for snake, slithering along,
T   is for television, to watch my favourite programmes.
U   is for underground, where moles live,
V   is for vision - my eyes which see.
W   is for a witch, flying on her broomstick,
X   is for xylophone, to play a tune.
Y   is for yellow, the colour of the sun,
Z   is for zebra, running wild.

Jordan Feetham (10)
St Theresa's RC Primary School

MY FAVOURITE THINGS

My favourite things are all around
They're floating everywhere
Will someone give them back to me
Before I lose my hair?

My teddy bears are on the roof
Ready to jump down
They're going to try and trick the queen
So that they can run off with her crown.

My baby doll is in the shop
Eating all the sweets
She hasn't paid for one tiny thing
Because she's poisoned them with her feet.

Now here they are -
Begging on their knees
They said, 'We'll be good, take us back please!'

Jade Poole (11)
St Theresa's RC Primary School

MR WELLY

Old Mr Welly was really smelly
he lived with his wife, down the lane.
His wife, he said, 'She gets on my head!'
but she said he was a pain!

His older daughter Telly, is also so smelly
and her belly is as big as her Dad's!
She eats lots of jelly on top of her belly
and says she's as mad as her dad.

And then there's the son - he drinks plenty of rum
when you see them together
locked up like a feather -
he's the worse one of the bunch!

Bradley Bradshaw (11)
St Theresa's RC Primary School

THE FAMILY

Mr Pork
Who lived in New York,
Went on a trip to Turkey.
He lost his wife
But she wasn't that nice,
So retired and moved to Mercury.

Mrs Pork
Who had a divorce,
Decided to find a new husband,
Her luck was so bad
Smoking was all that she had,
So retired and moved to Neverland.

Miss Pork
Who had a fat goat,
Decided to ship it to Asia.
The ship sunk at half-way
What more could she say,
Except that it was a total failure.

Amanda Caesar (11)
St Theresa's RC Primary School

PIPPIN THE PUPPET

Pippin is my favourite toy
A puppet from my youth.
He's beige and floppy, always cuddly
And dances to my tune.

He always stays right by my side
And sometimes likes to hide.
He always keeps you really warm
And snugly inside.

Pippin loves to entertain
He's ready with a smile,
My friends all love him, when they stay
To play with him all day.

Emma White (11)
St Theresa's RC Primary School

SCARY THINGS!

Are you scared of bogeymen?
I am.
Will you get scared if you're left alone?
I will.
Are you terrified of shadows?
I am.
Are you a fan of skeletons?
I'm not.
Are you a fan of mummies?
I'm not.
Scary things are all round us
All around!

Luke Platts (11)
St Theresa's RC Primary School

FAVOURITE THINGS

A   is for art equipment to make models
B   is for bowls to eat from
C   is for cash to buy stuff with
D   is for dolls to play with when I'm bored
E   is for eye make-up to dress up in
F   is for a football to kick to a friend
G   is for gel to scrape my hair back
H   is for handbag to carry around
I   is for ink to write a letter
J   is for jumper to put on when I'm cold
K   is for kickers - my best shoes
L   is for lunch to eat on the way
M   is for models to show my friends
N   is for nails to glue to my fingers
O   is for Octopus - my teddy
P   is for pepper to put on my dinner
Q   is for quilt to put over me at night
R   is for ring to put on my finger
S   is for string to do some sewing
T   is for toothbrush to clean my teeth
U   is for underwear to wear underneath
V   is for volcano - my funniest toy
W   is for watch so I know the time
X   is for xylophone to play some music
Y   is for yo-yo to roll up and down
Z   is for zip to sew on to my coat.

Chloe Lomas (10)
St Theresa's RC Primary School

FEARS

Fears, fears, fears
What are we without them?
Children lie awake at bedtime
It's just the way we're made.

Doors slam, floorboards creak,
I hear sounds around me.
Someone seems to be in the room
Or is it just *Mum?*

Emily Biney (10)
St Theresa's RC Primary School

SPIDER

I once had a spider
I named him George,
He drank some cider
Underneath the porch.

I'll never ever forget him,
He sleeps under the Land Rover,
But once my dad Tim
Went and ran him over.

Whitney Hill (10)
St Theresa's RC Primary School

PASHA'S PERFECT POEM

A is for amazing academy
B is for boys - annoying and horrible
C is for chocolate, melting in your mouth
D is for dogs, cute and cuddly
E is for elephants, big and grey.
F is for favourite things I like to keep
G is for glitter, which I put on my body
H is for hiding-and-seeking
I is for insects I don't like
J is for jumpers which I wear in the winter
K is for Kelly Rowland, my favourite singer
L is for lying on my bed
M is for monkeys, my best friend's favourite animal
N is for Neverland, a place to live in
O is for Oscar, my pet woodlouse
P is for Pasha, who is writing this poem.

Pasha Adele Ankers (10)
St Theresa's RC Primary School

THE TROLLEY MAN

There was an old man who lived in a trolley
He spent all his days holding a brolly
He thought it might rain
All his clothes would get stained
So he sat there, just sucking his lolly.

Charlotte Linfitt (11)
St Theresa's RC Primary School

MY FAVOURITE A-Z

A   is for anorak to keep out the rain
B   is for a bear, to sleep with at night
C   is for chocolate, which I love to eat
D   is for dinosaur, which I play with at night
E   is for envelopes, which I use to put my letters in
F   is for a friendship bracelet - kept safe all the time
G   is for a globe, which I look at at night
H   is for a hat to keep my head from the sun
I   is for inhaler which I always carry around with me
J   is for jumper, it keeps me warm if it's cold
K   is for Kellogg's Cornflakes for my breakfast
L   is for letters to write to my family
M   is for a monkey, to cuddle at night
N   is for newspapers to read in the morning
O   is for an orange, to eat after dinner
P   is for a pen to write some letters with
Q   is for question cards to test myself each day
R   is for a ruby, a beautiful ring
S   is for slippers to keep my feet warm
T   is for a telescope to look at the sun
U   is for an umbrella to keep me dry
V   is for a violin to play nice tunes on
W   is for a windmill, my little ornament
X   is for a xylophone to practise playing
Y   is for a yo-yo to use in the day
Z   is for zebra, my zebra-shaped box.

Terri Adkins (11)
St Theresa's RC Primary School

FRIEND

Friends are just like family,
They help you when you're down,
Make you smile when you're blue
They're honest, loyal and trustworthy.
Friends are cool,
They make you feel special,
Happy when they are around.
Having a friend is just like having a brother or sister,
They become your best friend for life,
You'll never be lonely while they're around.

Jade Lawson (11)
St Theresa's RC Primary School

THE PIED PIPER OF HAMELIN

The Piper smiled as he began to say,
'I will get my own way!'
The mayor frowned in dismay
As the Piper went on his way.

The Piper played his music sweet,
As the children tapped their feet.
The adults' voices drowned out by the beat
As the Piper and children went up the street.

The Piper lead the children into a cave
But only one child could be saved.
For he was one slow, lonely knave
No other child could be saved.

Loren Turner (10)
Southfield Primary School

MONKEYS

Monkeys are great all day long
On the branches they jump from tree to tree
Noisily yelling at their friends
Kicking their legs to help them along
Exercising their arms
Yawning, yelling noisily
Swinging through the trees.

Rachel Taylor (11)
Trinity Croft CE (A) School

A VIEW OF A HORSE

A horse runs fast
And gallops along,
A horse eats hay
And it has a loud *nay!*
A brown animal and so tall,
A brown beauty,
A horse is friendly though
A horse can be wild.
A horse can be for adults - tall
And for small children.

Nicole Cox (11)
Trinity Croft CE (A) School

ALIENS

A liens from out of space
L iving on Mars
I nvading Earth
E yes like a googly monster
N asty creatures
S melly, green, disgusting guys.

Robin Stanley (10)
Trinity Croft CE (A) School

CHEETAHS

C heetahs are spotty, fluffy and vast
H unting for delicious food, they run so fast
E very day, roaming round
E ating their food, not making a sound
T reading carefully, jumping high
A ll the time looking, no one comes close
H aving a doze
S hh! Don't wake me!

Bethan Middlemiss (10)
Trinity Croft CE (A) School

THE GOOGLY GLASS-EYED MONSTER

The glass-eyed, googly monster
Looked down from outer space
Within a splendid sparkly shock
He decided to run back to base
The glass-eyed, googly monster
Told his mum and dad
What a beautiful sight he'd seen
So when they came down to look
At the beautiful sight he'd seen
They had a party and flew a kite
And never since, have been seen.

Travis Cant (11)
Trinity Croft CE (A) School

A VIEW OF SCHOOL

S   chool is great until you have to do work which you don't like
C   hildren playing and shouting in the playground
H   owling children who don't work
O   utstanding work being done by children
O   ver the wall come children to get to school
L   aughing children play around.

Luke Wagstaff (10)
Trinity Croft CE (A) School

I Wonder . . .

I wonder what it's like to be a worm underground
I wonder what it's like to be a bird up above
I wonder what it's like to be a fish in the sea
I wonder what it's like to be a squirrel in the trees
I know what it's like to be a human . . . *like me!*

Jessica Connelly (10)
Victoria Primary School

The Test

I hope I'm going to be the best,
My heart is like a drum inside my chest.
I've got sweat on my palms,
I feel shivers in my arms.
I've been practising very hard,
My legs feel like lard.
What is this big pest?
It's the dreaded school test!

Brian Gillmore (11)
Victoria Primary School

MOON CREATURE

Moon creature, odd feature
Hair as long as a snake,
Teeth that can easily break,
Tail as long as my leg.
Arms that go up to its head,
Eyes as big as three eggs.
But skin dotty,
Scalp spotty.

Ashleigh Campbell (8)
Victoria Primary School

IMAGINE AN ELEPHANT

Imagine an elephant like a washing line
Imagine an elephant as tall as the sky
Imagine an elephant as cold as snow
Imagine an elephant like slate or stone
Imagine an elephant as fat as the globe
Imagine an elephant as hot as the sun
Imagine an elephant like a banner
Imagine an elephant as poisonous as a snake
Imagine an elephant as red as roses
Imagine an elephant like a block of flats
Imagine an elephant as black as night
Imagine an elephant as white as snow.

Connah Hunter (8)
Woodthorpe School

THE WINTER FAIRIES

Fairies gliding through the snow
All dressed in sparkling white
Passing through the winter's night
Wishing people well.

Children playing in the snow
Not seeing the fairies pass
There's one more night legend
Of winter, so let's make it last.

Emira Essalah (9)
Woodthorpe School